Lewisch/Posamentier

Mathematisches Fachwörterbuch

Ingrid Lewisch, Dr. phil. und Mag. rer. nat., studierte Mathematik und Physik an der Universität Wien. Professorin an der Pädagogischen Akademie des Bundes in Wien, Autorin vieler Schulbücher und fachdidaktischer Schriften für Mathematik und Physik.

Alfred S. Posamentier, M. A. and Ph. D., Professor of Mathematics Education and Deputy Dean of the School of Education of the City College of the City University of New York, author and coauthor of numerous mathematics books for teachers and secondary school students.

Ingrid Lewisch
Alfred S. Posamentier

Mathematisches Fachwörterbuch

Englisch – Deutsch
Deutsch – Englisch

R. Oldenbourg Verlag Wien 1996

© 1996 R. Oldenbourg Ges. m. b. H., Wien

Das Werk ist urheberrechtlich geschützt. Die dadurch begründeten Rechte, insbesondere die des Nachdrucks, der Wiedergabe auf fotomechanischem oder ähnlichem Wege sowie der Speicherung und Auswertung in Datenverarbeitungsanlagen, bleiben, auch bei nur auszugsweiser Verwertung, vorbehalten. Werden mit schriftlicher Einwilligung des Verlags einzelne Vervielfältigungsstücke für gewerbliche Zwecke hergestellt, ist an den Verlag die gesetzlich zu zahlende Vergütung zu entrichten, über deren Höhe der Verlag Auskunft gibt.

Zeichnungen: Dipl.-Ing. Elfriede Bammer

Umschlagentwurf: Katharina Uschan

Herstellung: Druckhaus Grasl, A-2540 Bad Vöslau

ISBN 3-7029-0708-4 R. Oldenbourg Wien
ISBN 3-486-24056-0 R. Oldenbourg München

Inhalt

1. Teil
Englisch – Deutsch 7

2. Teil
Deutsch – Englisch 33

3. Teil
Schreib- und Sprechweise mathematischer Ausdrücke 63
   Zahlen und Zahlenmengen 63
   Fachausdrücke der Rechenoperationen 64
   Sprechweise von Zahlenausdrücken 65
   Sprechweise von Rechenausdrücken 67
   Symbole aus der Mengenlehre und Logik 73
   Algebraische Strukturen 74
   Statistik 75
   Gerade, Strecke, Strahl 77
   Winkel 78
   Kongruenz und Ähnlichkeit 79
   Kreis 79
   Dreiecke 80
   Vierecke 82
   Vielecke 82
   Geometrische Körper 83
   Vektorrechnung 85
   Trigonometrie 86
   Analytische Geometrie 87

Anhang 89
   Maße und Gewichte 89
   Temperaturumrechnung 90
   Zahlwörter 91

Preface / Vorwort

In the past several years, it has become recognized that English is the most widely used international language. Today's students are encouraged to read as many English language books as possible.
To assist in this reading, there is a plethora of dictionaries, translation dictionaries, both in print and in electronic form. These are all fine for general reading. However, when one reads technical material, then a translator dictionary is needed since it provides words either not found in a general dictionary or gives the special technical uses of typical words.
This book is intended to provide support for people fluent in the German language reading English language mathematics books or books closely related to mathematics. Naturally, English speakers can also use this book as an aid to reading German mathematics books.
This book is divided into several parts. There is the English/German and German/English translation section, and a section of common mathematical expressions, so that a reader not only can read and understand the material, but also can learn to "say it correctly".
The book also takes into account the differences between British and American English.

*

In den letzten Jahren entwickelte sich Englisch immer mehr zur führenden internationalen Sprache. Besonders für Studenten von heute ist es daher notwendig, englische Fachliteratur lesen zu können.
Es gibt eine große Zahl von Wörterbüchern, und zwar sowohl in gedruckter als auch in elektronischer Form. Diese Wörterbücher sind zum Lesen von allgemein gehaltenen Texten geeignet. Für Spezialtexte ist jedoch ein Fachwörterbuch erforderlich.
Dieses Buch dient als Hilfe zum Lesen von Mathematikbüchern oder Büchern mit mathematisch verwandten Inhalten, die in englischer Sprache geschrieben sind. Natürlich können auch Englisch-Sprechende das Fachwörterbuch zum Lesen von deutschen Mathematikbüchern verwenden.
Das Buch ist in verschiedene Abschnitte unterteilt. Die beiden Hauptteile sind die Übersetzungen Englisch/Deutsch und Deutsch/Englisch. In einem weiteren Abschnitt sind Schreib- und Sprechweisen von mathematischen Ausdrücken und Redewendungen enthalten, so daß der Benützer einen Text nicht nur lesen und verstehen kann, sondern auch lernt „wie man es richtig sagt".
Auch auf die Unterschiede zwischen dem britischen und dem amerikanischen Englisch wird eingegangen.

The authors / Die Autoren

A. S. Posamentier, New York   Ingrid Lewisch, Wien

1. Teil
Englisch–Deutsch

A

ability   Fähigkeit, Befähigung
abscissa   Abszisse
absent   abwesend, fehlend
absolute   absolut, unbedingt
absolute cell (class) frequency   absolute Klassenhäufigkeit
absolute error   absoluter Fehler
absolute frequency   absolute Häufigkeit
absolute value   Betrag, Absolutbetrag, Absolutwert
acceleration   Beschleunigung
accentuate   betonen, hervorheben
accept   annehmen, akzeptieren
acceptable   annehmbar
accidental   zufällig, unbeabsichtigt
accompany   begleiten
accumulate   sich häufen, anhäufen
accumulation point   Häufungspunkt
accurate   genau, präzise
accustomed   gewöhnt
achieve   zustande bringen, erreichen, erledigen, leisten
achievement   Leistung, Erreichtes
achievement evaluation   Leistungsbeurteilung
achievement oriented   leistungsorientiert
acknowledgment   Anerkennung, Bestätigung
acquire   erlangen, sich aneignen (Wissen)
actual size   Istmaß, tatsächliches Maß
acute   spitz, scharf
acute angle   spitzer Winkel
acute triangle   spitzwinkliges Dreieck
add (add up)   summieren, addieren
addend   Summand
addition   Addition, Vermehrung
addition sign   Summenzeichen, Additionszeichen
addition table   Additionstabelle
adjacent   angrenzend, benachbart
adjacent angle   Nebenwinkel, anliegender Winkel
adjacent side   Ankathete
adjoin   (an)grenzen, beifügen
adjoint mapping   adjungierte Abbildung
adjoint matrix   adjungierte Matrix
advance   vorrücken, Fortschritte machen
affine map   affine Abbildung
affine space   affiner Raum
affinity   Affinität
age group   Jahrgang
aim   Ziel, Absicht
algebra   Algebra
algebra of sets   Mengenalgebra
algebraic   algebraisch
algebraic equation   algebraische Gleichung
algebraic expression   algebraischer Ausdruck
algebraic field extension   algebraische Körpererweiterung
algebraic number   algebraische Zahl
algebraic structure   algebraische Struktur
algebraically closed   algebraisch abgeschlossen
algorithm   Algorithmus
almost all   fast alle
alter   ändern
alternating   alternierend
alternating group   alternierende Gruppe
altitude   Höhe
ambiguous   zweideutig (unklar)
amount   Betrag, Höhe der Summe
amplitude   Amplitude, Schwingungsweite
analog computer   Analogrechner
analysis   Analysis
analysis of variance   Varianzanalyse
analytic function   analytische Funktion
analytic geometry   analytische Geometrie
analyze   analysieren, genau untersuchen
angle   Winkel
   acute angle   spitzer Winkel
   adjacent angle   anliegender Winkel
   exterior angle   Außenwinkel
   included angle   eingeschlossener Winkel
   interior angle   Innenwinkel
   obtuse angle   stumpfer Winkel
   opposite angle   gegenüberliegender Winkel
   reflex angle   erhabener Winkel

right angle rechter Winkel
straight angle gestreckter Winkel
angle bisector Winkelsymmetrale, Winkelhalbierende
angle of inclination Neigungswinkel
annually jährlich
annulus Ring, Kreisring
antecedent Vorderglied, Vorgänger, Vorgeschichte
anticipate erwarten, im voraus tun
anti-clockwise rotation Drehung entgegen dem Uhrzeigersinn (Linksdrehung)
antithesis Antithese
apex Gipfel, Spitze
apothem (of a polygon) Inkreisradius (eines regelmäßigen Vielecks)
application Gebrauch, Anwendung, Antrag
application-oriented examples anwendungsorientierte Beispiele
apply verwenden, anwenden
approach sich nähern, nahekommen
appropriate passend, geeignet, entsprechend
approximate annähernd, ungefähr
approximation Approximation, Näherung
arbitrarily (large/small) beliebig (groß/klein)
arbitrary willkürlich, eigenmächtig
arbitrary number unbestimmte Zahl
arc Bogen
arc cosecant Arkuskosekans
arc cosine Arkuskosinus
arc cotangent Arkuskotangens
arc length Länge des Kreisbogens
arc secant Arkussekans
arc sine Arkussinus
arc tangent Arkustangens
area Flächeninhalt, Fläche, Gebiet
lateral area Mantelfläche (Seitenfläche)
surface area Oberfläche, Oberflächeninhalt
area of a circle Kreisfläche, Flächeninhalt eines Kreises
area of a triangle (quadrilateral) Flächeninhalt eines Dreiecks (Vierecks)
argue erörtern, beweisen
argument Beweisgrund, Argument
arithmetic Arithmetik
arithmetic mean (average) arithmetisches Mittel, arithmetischer Durchschnitt

arithmetic operation Grundrechnungsart, Rechenoperation
arithmetic problem arithmetische Aufgabe, Rechenaufgabe
arithmetic progression arithmetische Progression
arithmetic sequence arithmetische Folge
arrangement Anordnung, Einteilung, Abmachung
arrangement according to magnitude Anordnung der Größe nach
arrangement in ascending (descending) powers Anordnung nach aufsteigenden (absteigenden) Potenzen
array Ordnung, Aufstellung, Anordnung, Verteilung
arrow Pfeil
arrowhead Pfeilspitze
ascend aufsteigen, ansteigen
ascending continued fraction aufsteigender Kettenbruch
ascending order aufsteigende Anordnung, aufsteigend geordnet
ascending powers aufsteigende (steigende, wachsende) Potenzen
ascending sequence wachsende Folge
assert behaupten, geltend machen
assertion Behauptung, Aussage
assess einschätzen, bewerten, besteuern
assessment Einschätzung, Bewertung
assign zuweisen, zuteilen
assignment Zuweisung, Aufgabe
associate verbinden, assoziieren
associative assoziativ
associative binary operation assoziative binäre (zweistellige) Operation
associative commutative ring assoziativer kommutativer Ring
associative law Assoziativgesetz, Verbindungsgesetz
associativity Assoziativität
assume annehmen, voraussetzen
assumption Annahme, Voraussetzung
asterisk (*) Stern, Sternchen
asteroid Astroide, Sternkurve
asymptote Asymptote
attain erreichen, erlangen
attainable erreichbar
attainable accuracy erreichbare Genauigkeit
attempt versuchen, probieren

attention Aufmerksamkeit
augment vermehren, vergrößern
augmented matrix erweiterte Matrix
authenticity Glaubwürdigkeit, Authentizität
automorphism Automorphismus
auxiliary helfend, Hilfs …
auxiliary calculation Nebenrechnung
auxiliary line Hilfslinie
auxiliary variable Hilfsvariable
available erhältlich, verfügbar
average Durchschnitt, Mittelwert
averaging Mittelung, Mittelwertbildung
averaging method Mittelungsmethode
avoid vermeiden, ausweichen
axiom of choice Auswahlaxiom
axiom of countability Abzählbarkeitsaxiom
axis (x-axis) Achse (x-Achse)
 imaginary axis imaginäre Achse
 major axis große Achse
 minor axis kleine Achse
 real axis reelle Achse
axis of symmetry Symmetrieachse, Spiegelungsachse

B

bar Stab, Stange, Balken
bar graph Balkendiagramm
base (basis) Basis, Grundlinie, Grundfläche, Grundzahl
basis vector Basisvektor, Grundvektor
bell-shaped curve Glockenkurve
benefit Vorteil, Nutzen, Gewinn
Bernoulli distribution Bernoulli-Verteilung, Binomialverteilung
beta error Fehler zweiter Art
better approximation bessere Näherung
between zwischen
biased sample verzerrte (verfälschte) Stichprobe
biconditional „genau dann, wenn", „↔"
bijective bijektiv, eineindeutig
bijective mapping bijektive (eineindeutige) Abbildung
bilateral zweiseitig
bilinear bilinear
bilinear form Bilinearform
billion *(Brit.)* Billion (10^{12})
billion *(Am.)* Milliarde (10^9)
binary binär, aus zwei Einheiten bestehend
binary code Binärcode
binary digit Binärziffer
binary number Binärzahl, Dualzahl
binary system Binärsystem, Zweiersystem
binomial binomial, zweinamig
binomial distribution Binomialverteilung
binomial expansion Binomialentwicklung
binomial series binomische Reihe
binomial theorem binomischer Lehrsatz
bisect halbieren, in zwei Teile schneiden
bisection Halbierung
bisector Halbierungslinie
bisector of an angle Winkelsymmetrale, Winkelhalbierende
body Körper
Boolean Algebra Boolesche Algebra
border Rand, Landesgrenze
bordering Umrandung
bound Schranke, Grenze; abgrenzen, beschränken
boundary Grenze, Begrenzung, Rand
bounded from above or below nach oben oder unten beschränkt
bounded interval beschränktes Intervall
bounded sequence beschränkte Folge
brace geschwungene Klammer
bracket eckige Klammer *(Am.)*, runde Klammer *(Brit.)*
branch Zweig
branch of hyperbola Hyperbelast
breadth Breite
break Abbruch, Knickstelle, Unstetigkeitsstelle
broken line Streckenzug
building block principle Bausteinprinzip
business arithmetic kaufmännische Arithmetik (Rechnen)
byte Byte

C

calculate berechnen, rechnen
calculation Rechnung
calculation of zeros of polynomials Nullstellenbestimmung bei Polynomen
calculation with powers Potenzrechnung
calculation with roots Wurzelrechnung
calculus Analysis, Kalkül

differential calculus Differentialrechnung
infinitesimal calculus Infinitesimalrechnung
integral calculus Integralrechnung
calculus of errors Fehlerrechnung
calculus of probabilities Wahrscheinlichkeitsrechnung
calipers Tasterzirkel, Greifzirkel
cancel kürzen, austreichen
capacity Inhalt, Volumen, Kapazität
cardinal (number) Kardinalzahl, Grundzahl
cardinality Mächtigkeit
Cartesian coordinate system kartesisches Koordinatensystem
Cartesian product kartesisches Produkt (von Mengen)
category Kategorie
catenary Kettenlinie
Cauchy's criterion for convergence Cauchysches Konvergenzkriterium
Cauchy-Riemann equations Cauchy-Riemannsche Differentialgleichungen
cell Klassenintervall, Zelle
cell frequency Klassenhäufigkeit
center (*Am.*), **centre** (*Brit.*) Mittelpunkt
center of gravity Schwerpunkt
centroid Schnittpunkt der Schwerlinien (Schwerpunkt)
century Jahrhundert
certain event sicheres Ereignis
chain Kette
chain rule Kettenregel
challenge Herausforderung, herausfordern
change in (of) sign Vorzeichenänderung
character Charakter, Buchstabe (Schriftzeichen)
characteristic Charakteristik
chart Karte, Tabelle, graphische Darstellung
check überprüfen, kontrollieren
check a calculation nachrechnen
checkerboard Damebrett, Schachbrett, Karomuster
checkered kariert
Chi-square distribution Chi-Quadrat-Verteilung
Chi-square test Chi-square-Test
Chinese remainder theorem Chinesischer Restsatz

chord (of a circle) Sehne (Kreissehne)
circle Kreis
  circumscribed circle umgeschriebener Kreis, Umkreis
  escribed circle angeschriebener Kreis, Ankreis
  inscribed circle eingeschriebener Kreis, Inkreis
  unit circle Einheitskreis
circle graph Kreisdiagramm
circular kreisförmig, rund
circular cone Kreiskegel
circular cylinder Kreiszylinder
circumcenter Umkreismittelpunkt
circumcircle Umkreis
circumference of a circle Umfang, Kreisumfang
circumradius Umkreisradius
closed abgeschlossen
closed map abgeschlossene Abbildung
closed set abgeschlossen Menge
closed with respect to an operation abgeschlossen bezüglich einer Verknüpfung
cluster point Häufungspunkt
coefficient Koeffizient
  undetermined coefficient unbestimmter Koeffizient
coin Münze
collapsible compasses zusammenfallender Zirkel
collection Sammlung
collinear points kollineare Punkte
collinearity Kollinearität
column Spalte (Kolonne)
combination Kombination
combination with (without) repetition Kombination mit (ohne) Wiederholung
combinatorial analysis Kombinatorik
combine kombinieren
comma Komma
commensurable kommensurabel, vergleichbar, mit gemeinsamem Maß
commensurate von gleicher Dauer wie, in Einklang stehend (mit), entsprechend
common gemeinsam
common denominator gemeinsamer Nenner
common divisor gemeinsamer Teiler
common multiple gemeinsames Vielfaches

common tangents gemeinsame Tangenten
commutative kommutativ
commutative field kommutativer Körper
commutative law Kommutativgesetz, Vertauschungsgesetz
commutativity Kommutativität
compare vergleichen
comparison of coefficients Koeffizientenvergleich
comparison test Vergleichskriterium (bei Reihen)
compass Kompaß
compasses (pair of) Zirkel
competency Befähigung, Tauglichkeit
complement Komplement, Ergänzung
complementary angle Komplementwinkel
complementary event entgegengesetztes Ereignis
complementary matrix komplementäre Matrix
completeness Vollständigkeit
completion Ergänzung
complex komplex, zusammengesetzt
complex field Körper der komplexen Zahlen
complex number komplexe Zahl
components Komponenten
composite number zusammengesetzte Zahl
compound interest Zinseszinsen
comprehend umfassen, begreifen, verstehen
comprehensive umfassend, inhaltsreich
compute rechnen
computer Rechner, Computer
computer science Computerwissenschaft, Informatik
computer scientist Informatiker
concentrate konzentrieren
concentric konzentrisch
concise kurz, knapp, prägnant
conclusion Schlußfolgerung, Ergebnis
concurrent durch denselben Punkt gehend
concyclic konzyklisch
conditional probability bedingte Wahrscheinlichkeit
conditionally convergent bedingt konvergent
cone Kegel
  circular cone Kreiskegel
  right cone gerader Kegel
  oblique cone schiefer Kegel
  truncated cone abgeschnittener Kegel
conic kegelförmig
conic section Kegelschnitt
conic surface Kegeloberfläche
confidence interval Konfidenzintervall
confidence region Konfidenzbereich
congruence Kongruenz
  triangle congruence theorems Kongruenzsätze für Dreiecke
congruent kongruent
congruent modulo m kongruent modulo m
congruent mapping Kongruenzabbildung
conjecture Vermutung
conjugated complex number konjugiert komplexe Zahl
conjunction Konjunktion, „und"–Operation
connected zusammenhängend
conscious bewußt
consider nachdenken, überlegen
consistency Widerspruchsfreiheit
constant Konstante
constant term konstantes Glied
constructibility Konstruierbarkeit
construction Konstruktion
contact Berührung
content(s) Inhalt
contiguity Berührung, Nähe, Nachbarschaft
continued fraction Kettenbruch
continuity Stetigkeit, Kontinuität
continuous stetig, kontinuierlich
continuous distribution stetige Verteilung
continuous process stetiger Prozeß
continuous progression stetige Progression
continuum Kontinuum
contradiction Widerspruch
contrapositive sentence Kontraposition, Umkehrung
contribute beitragen, beisteuern
converge konvergieren, streben
convergence Konvergenz
  uniform convergence gleichmäßige Konvergenz
convergence criteria Konvergenzkriterien
convergent konvergent
converse implication umgekehrte Implikation, Gegenimplikation, konverse Implikation

converse theorem Umkehrsatz
conversion Umrechnung
conversion of units Umwandlung von Maßeinheiten
conversion table Umrechnungstabelle
convert umrechnen, umwandeln
convex konvex
convex polygon konvexes Polygon
convolution Faltung
coordinate Koordinate
coordinate geometry Koordinatengeometrie
coordinate plane Koordinatenebene
coordinate system Koordinatensystem
coplanar lines komplanare (in einer Ebene liegende) Geraden
coplanarity Komplanarität
copy Exemplar, Abschrift, Kopie
core Kern
corner Eckpunkt, Ecke
corollary Korollar, Folgesatz
correction Korrektur, Verbesserung
correlation Korrelation, Wechselbeziehung, Zuordnung
correspondence (1–1 correspondence) Korrespondenz, Übereinstimmung (eineindeutige Abbildung)
corresponding entsprechend, gemäß
coset (or residue class) Restklasse (Nebenklasse)
cosine (cosine function) Kosinus (Kosinusfunktion)
cotangent (cotangent function) Kotangens (Kotangensfunktion)
count zählen
count backwards rückwärts zählen
countability Abzählbarkeit
countable abzählbar
counterclockwise entgegengesetzt zum Uhrzeigersinn, Gegenuhrzeigerrichtung
couple Paar
covariance analysis Kovarianzanalyse
covariant Kovariante
cover Überdeckung
coverage Reichweite, erfaßtes Gebiet, Geltungsbereich
covering Überdeckung, Überlagerung
criterion Kriterium, Maßstab
criterion for divisibility Teilbarkeitskriterium

cross Kreuz, kreuzen
cross-hatching Schraffierung
cross product Kreuzprodukt, vektorielles Produkt, äußeres Produkt
cross section Querschnitt
cube Würfel, kubieren, erheben in die dritte Potenz
cubic equation Gleichung dritten Grades
cubic measure Raummaß
cubic unit Vomumseinheit
cuboid Quader
curvature Krümmung (einer Kurve, einer Fläche)
curve integral Kurvenintegral
curve of the third degree Kurve dritten Grades
curvilinear correlation nichtlineare Korrelation
cusp Rückkehrpunkt, Scheitelpunkt, Rückkehrspitze
cut Schnitt
cyclic zyklisch, periodisch
cyclic group zyklische Gruppe
cyclic permutation zyklische Permutation
cyclic points Kreispunkte
cyclic quadrilateral eingeschriebenes Viereck
cycloid Zykloide
cyclotomic equation Kreisteilungsgleichung
cylinder Zylinder
cylindrical surface Zylinderoberfläche

D

dashed strichliert
data Daten
dearth Mangel
decade Dekade, Jahrzehnt, Zehnergruppe
decagon Dekagon, Zehneck
decahedron Dekaeder, Zehnflächner
decimal Dezimal ...
  repeating decimal periodische Dezimalzahl
decimal expansion Dezimalbruchentwicklung
decimal fraction Dezimalbruch
decimal number Dezimalzahl
decimal place Dezimalstelle
decimal point Dezimalpunkt, Komma

decimal system Dezimalsystem
decipher entziffern, enträtseln
decision Entscheidung
decode dekodieren, entschlüsseln
decomposition Zerlegung
decreasing fallend
decreasing progression fallende Progression
Dedekind cut Dedekindscher Schnitt
deduction Abzug, Preisnachlaß, Schlußfolgerung
deductive proof deduktiver Beweis
deficiency Mangel (an), Fehlen (von)
define definieren
definition Definition
  unambiguous definition eindeutige Definition
degree (order) Grad (Ordnung)
degree of an angle Winkelgrad
degrees of freedom Freiheitsgrade
delete (aus)streichen
denominator Nenner
  common denominator gemeinsamer Nenner
  least common denominator kleinster gemeinsamer Nenner
density Dichte
denumerable abzählbar
dependent abhängig
dependent variable abhängige Variable
depth Tiefe
derivable ableitbar, beweisbar
derivative Ableitung, Differentialquotient
  partial derivative partielle Ableitung
derivative of order first Ableitung erster Ordnung
descendant Nachfolger, Nachkommender
descending order fallende Anordnung
descriptive statistics beschreibende Statistik
design Entwurf, Plan, entwerfen, skizzieren
designation Bezeichnung
desirable wünschenswert, erwünscht
determinant (of the *n*-th order) Determinante (*n*-ter Ordnung)
develop entwickeln
development Entwicklung, Durchführung
deviation Abweichung
  standard deviation Standardabweichung
deviation from the mean Abweichung vom Mittelwert

diagonal Diagonale
diagonal matrix Diagonalmatrix
diagonalization of matrices Hauptachsentransformation von Matrizen
diagram Diagramm
  bar diagram Balkendiagramm
  circle diagram Kreisdiagramm
  line diagram Liniendiagramm
  scatter diagram Streuungsdiagramm, Punktwolke
diameter Durchmesser
difference Unterschied, Differenz
differentiability Differenzierbarkeit
differential Differential
differential and integral calculus Differential- und Integralrechnung
differentiate differenzieren, ableiten
differentiation Differentiation
  partial differentiation partielle Differentiation
differentiation rule Ableitungsregel
digit Ziffer, Stellenwert
  three-digit number dreistellige Zahl
digital computer Digitalrechner
digression Abweichung
dihedral angle Schnittwinkel zweier Ebenen bzw. Kanten
Diophantine equation Diophantische Gleichung
direct direkt
direct proof direkter Beweis
directed line segment gerichtete Strecke
direction Richtung
directrix Leitlinie, Leitgerade, Leitkurve
discontinuous unstetig
discount (rate) Diskont, Preisnachlaß (Diskontsatz)
discrete diskret
discrete variable diskrete Zufallsvariable
discriminant Diskriminante
disjoint sets disjunkte Mengen, elementfremde Mengen
dispersion Streuung
displace verschieben, verrücken
dissection Zerlegung
distance Distanz, Entfernung, Abstand
distinct verschieden
distortion Verzerrung
distribution Verteilung
  binomial distribution Binomialverteilung

continuous distribution stetige Verteilung
exponential distribution Exponentialverteilung
geometric distribution geometrische Verteilung
normal distribution Normalverteilung, Gauß-Verteilung
uniform distribution gleichmäßige Verteilung
distributive law Distributivgesetz
disturb stören, beunruhigen
divergence Divergenz
divergent divergent
divide (by) teilen, dividieren (durch)
dividend Dividend
divisibility Teilbarkeit
division Division, Teilung
division with remainder Divison mit Rest
divisor Divisor, Teiler
common divisor gemeinsamer Teiler
greatest common divisor größter gemeinsamer Teiler
dodecagon Dodekagon, Zwölfeck
dodecahedron Dodekaeder, Zwölfflächner
domain Bereich (algebraischer), Definitionsbereich, Gebiet
domain of convergence Konvergenzbereich
domain of a function Definitionsbereich einer Funktion
domain of integrity Integritätsbereich
dot product inneres Produkt (Skalarprodukt)
dotted punktiert
double doppelt, zweifach
double cone Doppelkegel
draw ziehen, zeichnen
draw a parallel to eine Parallele ziehen zu
drawing with (without) replacement Ziehen mit (ohne) Zurücklegen
drill Übung
duality principle Dualitätsprinzip
duplication Verdopplung
duplication of a cube Würfelverdopplung

E

eccentricity Exzentrizität
edge Kante
lateral edge Seitenkante
efficiency Wirksamkeit, Effizienz, Leistungsfähigkeit
eight (eighth) acht (achte)
eighteen (eighteenth) achtzehn (achtzehnte)
eighth Achtel
eighty (eightieth) achtzig (achtzigste)
element Element
neutral element neutrales Element
unit element Einheitselement
elevation Erhebung, Hebung, Aufriß
eleven (eleventh) elf (elfte)
eleventh Elftel
elimination Elimination, Beseitigung
process of elimination Eliminationsverfahren
elimination by comparison Gleichsetzungsverfahren
emerge auftauchen, hervorkommen
empirical expectation empirische Erwartung
empirical variance empirische Varianz
employ beschäftigen, einsetzen, benützen, anstellen
empty set leere Menge
end point Endpunkt
enrichment Bereicherung
entire ganz, völlig, vollkommen, unversehrt, uneingeschränkt
entire function ganze Funktion
envelope Einhüllende, einhüllen
envelope of a curve Hüllkurve
environment Umgebung
equal gleich
equal angles gleiche Winkel
equality Gleichheit
equate gleichsetzen
equate to zero Null setzen
equation Gleichung
indeterminate equation unbestimmt Gleichung
linear equation lineare Gleichung
quadratic equation quadratische Gleichung
radical equation Wurzelgleichung
equation in standard form Gleichung in Normalform
equation of the n-th degree Gleichung n-ten Grades
equation with two variables Gleichung in zwei Variablen

equiangular gleichwinkelig
equilateral gleichseitig
equipment Ausrüstung, Ausstattung, Gerät
equivalence Gleichwertigkeit, Äquivalenz
equivalence class Äquivalenzklasse
equivalence relation Äquivalenzrelation
erase ausradieren, löschen
error Fehler
error analysis Fehleranalyse
error approximation Fehlerabschätzung
error of observation Meßfehler, Beobachtungsfehler
escribed circle angeschriebener Kreis
establish einführen
estimate (ab-, ein)schätzen
estimation Abschätzung, Schätzwert
Euclidean division algorithm Euklidischer Algorithmus
Euclidean geometry Euklidische Geometrie
Euler line Eulersche Gerade
Euler number Eulersche Zahl
evaluate auswerten, berechnen
evaluation Berechnung, Beurteilung, Auswertung, Evaluierung
even gerade
  even number gerade Zahl
  function of even degree gerade Funktion
event Ereignis
evidence Beweis, Beweismittel
examination Prüfung, Test
example Beispiel
excircle (escribed circle) Ankreis (angeschriebener Kreis)
exhibit ausstellen, zeigen
expansion Entwicklung, Ausbreitung, Ausdehnung
  binomial expansion Binomialentwicklung
  decimal expansion Dezimalbruchentwicklung
expectation Erwartung
explanation Erklärung
explore erforschen, untersuchen
exponent Exponent, Hochzahl
exponential distribution Exponentialverteilung
exponential function Exponentialfunktion
expose aussetzen
express ausdrücken
expression Ausdruck
  algebraic expression algebraischer Ausdruck

extend (aus)dehnen, erweitern
extension Ausdehnung
exterior Äußeres
exterior angle Außenwinkel
exterior derivative äußere Ableitung
exterior point äußerer Punkt (Teilungspunkt)
external außen
externally tangent außenberührend
extreme extrem
extreme value Extremwert
extreme with auxiliary conditions Extremum mit Nebenbedingungen
extremes (term of a proportion) Außenglieder (einer Proportion)
extremity Ende, Endpunkt

F

***F*-distribution** *F*-Verteilung
***F*-test** *F*-Test
face Gesicht, Fläche, Außenfläche
face angle Flächenwinkel
face of a solid Seitenfläche
factor Faktor
  common factor gemeinsamer Faktor
  greatest common factor größter gemeinsamer Faktor
factor module Restklassenmodul
factor ring Restklassenring
factorable in Faktoren zerlegbar
factorial Fakultät, faktorielle
factoring Zerlegung
factorization into prime factors Primfaktorenzerlegung
failure Versagen, Mißerfolg
fair einigermaßen gut, nicht übel, gerecht, mittelmäßig
fallacy Trugschluß, Irrtum
false falsch
family Familie, Verwandtschaft, Schar
family of curves Kurvenschar, Kurvensystem
fault Fehler
favorable günstig
favorable event günstiges Ereignis
fiber Faser
Fibonacci sequence Fibonacci Folge
field algebraischer Körper, Feld
field extension Körpererweiterung

fifteen (fifteenth) fünfzehn (fünfzehnte)
fifth Fünftel
fifty (fiftieth) fünfzig (fünfzigste)
figure Ziffer, Figur
finite endlich
finite population endliche Grundgesamtheit
finite series endliche Reihe
finite-difference method Differenzenverfahren
first erste(r)
first term Anfangsglied
firstly erstens
five (fifth) fünf (fünfte)
five times fünfmal
fixed point representation Festkommadarstellung
flat rate Pauschalgebühr
floating point representation Gleitkommadarstellung
focal distance (in conics) Brennpunktabstand (bei Kegelschnittlinien)
focal radius Brennstrahl
focus (in conics) Brennpunkt (bei Kegelschnittlinien)
fold falten
foot of a perpendicular Fußpunkt des Lotes
form Form, Gestalt
formula Formel
  quadratic formula Lösungsformel für quardratische Gleichungen
forty (fortieth) vierzig (vierzigste)
foster fördern, begünstigen, unterstützen
four (fourth) vier (vierte)
fourfold vierfach
fourteen (fourteenth) vierzehn (vierzehnte)
fourth Viertel
fraction Bruch, Bruchteil
  improper fraction unechter (uneigentlicher) Bruch
  partial fraction Partialbruch
  proper fraction echter Bruch
  rational fraction rationaler Bruch
  reduced fraction gekürzter Bruch
fraction bar Bruchstrich
fraction in lowest terms gekürzter Bruch
fractional equation Bruchgleichung
fractional exponent gebrochener Exponent

frame Rahmen
frequency Häufigkeit
frequency curve Häufigkeitskurve
frequency distribution Häufigkeitsverteilung
frequency ratio relative Häufigkeit
frequency table Häufigkeitstabelle
frontier (boundary) Rand
frustum of a cone Kegelstumpf
frustum of a pyramid Pyramidenstumpf
function Funktion
  constant function konstante Funktion
  continuous function stetige Funktion
  domain of a function Definitionsbereich einer Funktion
  graph of a function Funktionsgraph
  range of a function Wertebereich einer Funktion
  reciprocal function reziproke Funktion
  recursive function rekursive Funktion
  term of a function Funktionsterm
function of even degree gerade Funktion
function of odd degree ungerade Funktion
function of one variable Funktion einer Variablen
function of several variables Funktion mehrerer Variabler
function theory Funktionstheorie
functional funktional
functional dependence funktionale Abhängigkeit
functional symbol Funktionssymbol, Operationszeichen
fundamental fundamental, grundlegend
fundamental concept Grundbegriff
fundamental group Fundamentalgruppe
fundamental integral Grundintegral
fundamental set Grundmenge
Fundamental Theorem of Algebra Fundamentalsatz der Algebra
Fundamental Theorem of Calculus Fundamentalsatz der Differential- und Integralrechnung

G

Galois theory Galois Theorie
gap Lücke
Gaussian elimination Gaußsches Eliminationsverfahren

generate   entwickeln, erzeugen
generating function   erzeugende Funktion
geometric   geometrisch
geometric distribution   geometrische Verteilung
geometric mean (average)   geometrisches Mittel
geometric progression   geometrische Progression
geometric sequence   geometrische Folge
geometric series   geometrische Reihe
geometry   Geometrie
  coordinate geometry   Koordinatengeometrie
  hyperbolic geometry   hyperbolische Geometrie
  projective geometry   projektive Geometrie
given   gegeben
goal   Ziel
golden section (ratio)   Goldener Schnitt
grain   Spur, ein Körnchen
graph   Diagramm, Graph
graph paper   Millimeterpapier, grafisches Papier
graphic solution   grafische Lösung
great circle of a sphere   Großkreis, Hauptkreis der Kugelfläche
greater than (>)   größer als
greater than or equal to (≥)   größer oder gleich
greatest common divisor   größter gemeinsamer Teiler
greatest common factor   größter gemeinsamer Faktor
greatest lower bound   untere Grenze, größte untere Schranke
gross earnings   Bruttoeinkommen
group   Gruppe
  alternating group   alternierende Gruppe
  cyclic group   zyklische Gruppe
  fundamental group   Fundamentalgruppe
group with respect to addition   Gruppe bezüglich der Addition
growth   Wachstum, Zunahme
guess   erraten, vermuten, schätzen

H

half   Hälfte, halbieren
half plane   Halbebene
half space   Halbraum
harmonic   harmonisch
harmonic mean   harmonisches Mittel
harmonic sequence   harmonische Folge
hatching   Schraffierung
heads or tails   Kopf oder Zahl (*Österr.* Kopf oder Adler)
height   Höhe
hemisphere   Halbkugel
heptagon   Siebeneck
heuristic   Heuristik
hexagon   Sechseck
hexahedron   Sechsflächner, Hexaeder
hint   Hinweis
histogram   Histogramm, Staffelbild
homogeneous system   homogenes Gleichungssystem
homomorphism   Homomorphismus
horizontal projection   Grundriß
Horner's method   Horner-Schema
howler   Heuler, grober Schnitzer
hundred (hundredth)   hundert (hundertste)
hundredth   Hundertstel
hyperbola   Hyperbel
hyperbolic   hyperbolisch
hyperbolic function   Hyperbelfunktion, hyperbolische Funktion
hyperbolic geometry (Lobachevskian)   hyperbolische Geometrie (Lobatschewskische)
hypotenuse   Hypotenuse
hypothesis   Hypothese

I

icosahedron   Zwanzigflächner, Ikosaeder
identity   Identität, identische Gleichheit
identity element   Einselement, Einheitselement
identity matrix   Einheitsmatrix
illusory correlation   Scheinkorrelation
imaginary   imaginär
imaginary axis   imaginäre Achse
imaginary number   imaginäre Zahl
imaginary part   Imaginärteil
imaginary root   imaginäre Wurzel
impact   Anprall, Aufschlag, Stoß, Effekt, Wirkung
implement   Werkzeug, Gerät, durchführen
implication   Implikation, Folgerung

imply implizieren, andeuten
improbable unwahrscheinlich
improper ungeeignet, unecht
improper fraction unechter Bruch, uneigentlicher Bruch
improper integral uneigentliches Integral
improve verbessern (Kenntnisse)
inaccessible unzugänglich
incenter *(Am.)*, **incentre** *(Brit.)* Inkreismittelpunkt
included angle eingeschlossener Winkel
income tax Einkommensteuer, Lohnsteuer
incommensurable inkommensurabel, ohne gemeinsames Maß
incompatible unverträglich
inconsistency Widersprüchlichkeit, Unvereinbarkeit, Unbeständigkeit
inconsistent equations unlösbare (unverträgliche) Gleichungen
increase Steigerung, Erhöhung, zunehmen, vergrößern
increasing function wachsende Funktion, steigende Funktion
indefinite integral unbestimmtes Integral
independent unabhängig
independent events unabhängige Ereignisse
independent variable unabhängige Variable
indeterminate equation unbestimmte Gleichung
indeterminate system of equations unbestimmtes Gleichungssystem
index set Indexmenge
indirect indirekt
indirect proof indirekter Beweis, Widerspruchsbeweis
induction Induktion
inequality Ungleichheit
inequality sign Ungleichheitszeichen
infinity Unendlichkeit
initial anfänglich
initial point Anfangspunkt
injective injektiv
inner product (dot product) inneres Produkt, Skalarprodukt
innumerable unzählbar
input Eingabe
inradius Inkreisradius
inscribe einschreiben
inscribed circle eingeschriebener Kreis, Inkreis

inscribed triangle (quadrilateral) eingeschriebenes Dreieck (Viereck)
insert einfügen
insertion Einfügung
insoluble unlösbar
insolvable unlösbar
inspect untersuchen
instructions Vorschrift, Anweisung
insurance statistics Versicherungsstatistik
integer ganze Zahl, ganzzahlig
integral Integral
  definite integral bestimmtes Integral
  improper integral uneigentliches Integral
  indefinite Integral unbestimmtes Integral
integral calculus Integralrechnung
integral domain Integritätsbereich (Ring)
integral number ganze Zahl, ganzzahlig
integrate integrieren
integration Integration
integration by parts partielle Integration
integration technique Integrationsmethode
intercept Abschnitt
  x-intercept Abschnitt auf der x-Achse
intercepted arc eingeschlossener Bogen
interest Zinsen, Gewinn, Interesse
interest rate (4 % interest) Zinssatz (4 % Zinsen)
interior Inneres
interior angle Innenwinkel
interior point innerer Punkt (Teilungspunkt)
internal tangency Berührung von innen
interpolation Interpolation, Einschalten von Zwischenwerten
intersecting lines (planes) sich schneidende Geraden (Ebenen)
intersecting sets Schnittmengen
intersection (point) Schnittpunkt
  point of intersection of the diagonals Diagonalenschnittpunkt
interval Intervall
  bounded interval beschränktes Intervall
  closed interval abgeschlossenes Intervall
  open interval offenes Intervall
  unbounded interval unbeschränktes Intervall
introduce einführen, einleiten
introduction Einführung, Einleitung
invariant invariant, unveränderlich
invention Erfindung

inventive erfinderisch
inventory Bestandsaufnahme
inverse invers, reziprok, umgekehrt
inverse image Urbild
inverse matrix inverse Matrix
inverse of a theorem Umkehrsatz, Umkehrtheorem, Kehrsatz
inverse proportional indirekt proportional
inverse sentence (proposition) konträre Aussage
inverse theorem Umkehrsatz
inverse trigonometric function inverse trigonometrische Funktion (Arcusfunktion)
inverse value inverser Wert, Kehrwert, reziproker Wert
inversion formula Umkehrformel
invertible invertierbar, umkehrbar
investigate untersuchen, erforschen
iota Jota
irrational irrational
irrational number irrationale Zahl
isolated point isolierter Punkt
isomorphism Isomorphismus
isosceles triangle gleichschenkeliges Dreieck

J

join verbinden, teilnehmen
jump Sprung, Sprungstelle
juxtaposition Stellen vertauschen (auswechseln)

K

kite Deltoid, Drachenviereck
klein's four group Kleinsche Vierergruppe
knowledge Wissen

L

label Beschriftung, beschriften
lack (of) Mangel (an)
Laplace expansion of a determinant Laplacescher Entwicklungssatz
last digit letzte Ziffer, Endziffer
last term letztes Glied, Endglied

lateral seitlich
lateral area (or surface) Mantelfläche, Seitenfläche
lateral edge Seitenkante
lateral surface Seitenfläche
lateral surface of a cone Kegelmantel
lattice Gitter
lattice point Gitterpunkt
law Gesetz
  associative law Assoziativgesetz (Verbindungsgesetz)
  commutative law Kommutativgesetz (Vertauschungsgesetz)
  distributive law Distributivgesetz (Verteilungsgesetz)
law of cosines Kosinussatz
law of inertia Trägheitsgesetz
law of large numbers Gesetz großer Zahlen
law of logic Gesetz der Logik
law of negation Verneinungsgesetz
law of sines Sinussatz
law of tangents Tangentensatz
leading coefficient höchster Koeffizient
leading term Glied mit dem höchsten Exponenten, Leitglied
leap year Schaltjahr
least common denominator kleinster gemeinsamer Nenner, Hauptnenner
least common multiple kleinstes gemeinsames Vielfaches
least squares method Methode der kleinsten Quadrate
least upper bound kleinste obere Schranke
left links
left hand parenthesis linke Klammer
leg Schenkel, Kathete
  adjacent leg Ankathete
  opposite leg Gegenkathete
Legendre equation Legendresche Differentialgleichung
length Länge
length of a side Seitenlänge
length of an altitude Länge der Höhe
length of an arc Bogenlänge
less than or equal to ($\leq$) kleiner oder gleich
level Niveau
level of significance Signifikanzniveau
lexicographic order lexikografische Ordnung
like gleich
like operation gleichnamige Operation

like power   gleiche Potenz (Glied)
like term   gleichnamiger Term
limit   Grenzwert, Limes
   lower limit   unterer Grenzwert
   upper limit   oberer Grenzwert
limit theorems   Grenzwertsätze
limited   begrenzt
line   Gerade, Linie
   auxiliary line   Hilfslinie
   dashed line   strichlierte Linie
   dotted line   punktierte Linie
   parallel line   parallele Gerade
   perpendicular line   normale Gerade
   skew line   windschiefe Gerade
   solid line   ausgezogene Linie
line graph   Liniendiagramm
line segment   Strecke
line symmetry   Symmetriegerade
linear   linear, geradlinig
linear algebra   lineare Algebra
linear combination   Linearkombination
linear equation   lineare Gleichung
linear mapping   lineare Abbildung
linear measure   Längenmaß
linear regression   lineare Regression
linearly dependent   linear abhängig
linearly independent   linear unabhängig
locus (geometric)   geometrischer Ort
log-log paper   doppelt logarithmisches Papier, Potenzpapier
logarithm (natural)   Logarithmus (natürlicher)
logarithm table   Logarithmentafel
logarithmic curve   logarithmische Kurve
logarithmic equation   logarithmische Gleichung
logarithmic spiral   logarithmische Spirale
logical consistency   Folgerichtigkeit
logical deduction   logischer Schluß
longevity   Langlebigkeit
loop   Schlinge, Schleife
loss of information   Informationsverlust
lower bound   untere Schranke
lower limit   unterer Limes, untere Grenze
lower sum   Untersumme

M

machine number   Maschinenzahl
magic square   magisches Quadrat
manifold   Mannigfaltigkeit
many to many mapping   mehrmehrdeutige Abbildung
mapping   Abbildung, Zuordnung
   adjoint mapping   adjungierte Abbildung
   affine mapping   affine Abbildung
   bijective mapping   bijektive (eineindeutige) Abbildung
   closed mapping   abgeschlossene Abbildung
   congruent mapping   Kongruenzabbildung
   linear mapping   lineare Abbildung
margin   Rand, Seitenrand
marginal distribution   Randverteilung
mark-off   abschlagen
masterly   meisterhaft, meisterlich
mastery   Herrschaft, Beherrschung, Überlegenheit
match   passen
math (*Am.*), **maths** (*Brit.*)   Mathe (Mathematik)
mathematical   mathematisch
mathematical analysis   Analysis
mathematical induction   vollständige Induktion
mathematician   Mathematiker(in)
mathematics   Mathematik
   higher mathematics   höhere Mathematik
matrix   Matrix
   adjoint matrix   adjungierte Matrix
   augmented matrix   erweiterte Matrix
   complementary matrix   komplementäre Matrix
   diagonal matrix   Diagonalmatrix
   identity matrix   Einheitsmatrix
   inverse matrix   inverse Matrix
   singular matrix   singuläre Matrix
matrix algebra   Matrizenalgebra
matrix notation   Matrixschreibweise
matrix representation   Matrixdarstellung
matrix transformation   Matrixtransformation
mature   reif, entwickelt, erwachsen
maximum point   Maximum, Hochpunkt
mean   Mittelwert
   arithmetic mean   arithmetischer Mittelwert
   geometric mean   geometrischer Mittelwert
   harmonic mean   harmonischer Mittelwert
mean curvature   mittlere Krümmung

mean proportional mittlere Proportionale
mean square deviation mittlere quadratische Abweichung
mean value theorem for integrals Mittelwertsatz der Integralrechnung
measure Maß, Maßeinheit, messen
measurement error Meßfehler
medial mittlere
median Median, Zentralwert
median (line) Halbierungslinie, Schwerlinie
member Mitglied
mental calculation Kopfrechnen
mention Erwähnung, erwähnen, betonen
method Methode
   least squares method Methode der kleinsten Quadrate
method of approach Näherungsmethode
method of undetermined coefficients Methode der unbestimmten Koeffizienten
metric space metrischer Raum
middle Mitte
midpoint Mittelpunkt, Halbierungspunkt
millennium Jahrtausend
minimal minimal, Mindest ...
minimum point Minimum, Tiefpunkt
minuend Minuend
minus sign Minuszeichen
mirror Spiegel, spiegeln
mirror image Spiegelbild
miscalculate verrechnen
missing value fehlender Wert
mistake Irrtum, Fehler
mixed number gemischte Zahl
mode Modus
moderately good einigermaßen gut
module Modul
monotone monoton
monotonically decreasing sequence monoton abnehmende Folge
monotonically increasing sequence monoton wachsende Folge
motion Bewegung
multinomial expansion Polynomialentwicklung
multiple Vielfaches
   least common multiple kleinstes gemeinsames Vielfaches
multiplication Multiplikation
multiplication table Einmaleins
multiply multiplizieren

mutual gegenseitig, wechselseitig
mutually exclusive events sich gegenseitig ausschließende Ereignisse

N

***n*-gon** *n*-Eck
natural logarithm natürlicher Logarithmus
natural number natürliche Zahl
naught Null
necessary (condition) notwendig, nötig (Bedingung)
negation Negation
negative negativ
negative numbers negative Zahlen
neighborhood Umgebung
Neil's parabola Neilsche Parabel
nested intervals Intervallschachtelung
nesting Schachtelung
net Netz
net earnings Nettoeinkommen
neutral element neutrales Element
Newton's method of approximation Newtonsches Näherungsverfahren
nine (ninth) neun (neunte)
nineteen (nineteenth) neunzehn (neunzehnte)
ninety (ninetieth) neunzig (neunzigste)
ninth Neuntel
non-degenerate conic nichtarteter Kegelschnitt
non-Euclidean geometry Nicht-Euklidische Geometrie
non-zero von Null verschieden
nonparallel nichtparallel
norm Norm
normal normal, lotrecht, senkrecht
normal distribution Normalverteilung, Gauß-Verteilung
normal form Normalform
normal order natürliche Reihenfolge
normalized polynomial normiertes Polynom
notation Schreibweise, Bezeichnung
null hypothesis Nullhypothese
null set leere Menge
number Zahl, Nummer (Adresse)
   algebraic number algebraische Zahl
   complex number komplexe Zahl
   decimal number Dezimalzahl

imaginary number imaginäre Zahl
integral number ganze Zahl, ganzzahlig
negative number negative Zahl
perfect number perfekte Zahl
prime number Primzahl
radical number Wurzelzahl
random number Zufallszahl
rational number rationale Zahl
real number reelle Zahl
undetermined number unbestimmte Zahl
whole number ganze Zahl
number line Zahlengerade
number of revolutions Umlaufzahl
number ray Zahlenstrahl
number theory Zahlentheorie
number triple (primitive) Zahlentripel (teilerfremdes)
numerator Zähler
numerical numerisch, zahlenmäßig
numerical differentiation numerische Differentiation
numerical integration numerische Integration
numerical order Zahlenfolge
numerical value Zahlenwert

O

objective sachlich, vorurteilslos, Ziel
oblique schief
  oblique solid Schiefkörper
observation Beobachtung
obtuse stumpf
obtuse angle stumpfer Winkel
obtuse triangle stumpfwinkliges Dreieck
occupation Besetzung, Beschäftigung, Beruf
occupy besetzen, belegen, beschäftigen
octagon Achteck, Oktagon
octahedron Achtflächner, Oktaeder
octal notation Oktalschreibweise
odd ungerade
odd number ungerade Zahl
once einmal
one eins
one-to-one correspondence umkehrbar eindeutige Beziehung
one-to-one mapping eineindeutige Abbildung
one-way classification Klassifizierung nach einem einzigen Merkmal

onto function surjektive Abbildung
open curve offene Kurve
operation Tätigkeit, Arbeitsvorgang
  arithmetical operation Grundrechnungsart, Rechenoperation
  inverse operation rückgängig machende Rechenoperation
  like operation gleichnamige Operation
operation with fractions Bruchrechnung
opposite gegenüberliegend, entgengerichtet, gegenüber, Gegenteil, Gegensatz
opposite angle Gegenwinkel, Scheitelwinkel
opposite sign entgegengesetztes Vorzeichen
opposite vector engegengesetzter Vektor
opposite vertex (of a quadrilateral) gegenüberliegender Eckpunkt (bei einem Viereck)
optimization Optimierung
order Ordnung
  random order zufällige Reihenfolge
  reverse order in umgekehrter Reihenfolge
ordered pair geordnetes Paar
ordinal number Ordnungszahl, Ordinalzahl
ordinary differential equation gewöhnliche Differntialgleichung
ordinate Ordinate
orientation Orientierung
origin (point) Anfangspunkt, Ursprung
origin of a coordinate plane Koordinatenursprung
orthocenter Höhenschnittpunkt
orthogonal orthogonal, senkrecht
oscillation Schwankung, Oszillation
osculating plane Schmiegeebene
outer Äußeres, Außen ...
outer product of vectors äußeres Produkt von Vektoren
outline Umriß, Überblick
output Ausgabe, Leistung, Produktion
overlap überlappen, übergreifen
overlay belegen, überlagern
overview Überblick

P

palindromic number palindrome Zahl
parabola Parabel
parabolic curve parabolische Kurve

parabolic surface parabolische Fläche
paradox Paradoxon
parallel parallel, Parallele
parallel displacement Parallelverschiebung
parallel lines parallele Geraden
parallel translation Parallelverschiebung
parallelepiped Parallelepiped, Parallelflach, Spat
parallelism Parallelität
parallelogram Parallelogramm
parameter Parameter
parametric curve Kurve in Parameterdarstellung
parametric equation Gleichung in Parameterdarstellung
parenthesis (*pl.* **parentheses**) *(Am.)* runde Klammer(n)
parity Parität, Gleichheit
partial partiell, teilweise
partial derivative partielle Ableitung, partieller Differentialquotient
partial differentiation partielle Differentiation
partial fraction Partialbruch
partial fraction expansion Partialbruchzerlegung
partial ordering Halbordnung
partial sum Partialsumme
partition (into classes) Klasseneinteilung
Pascal's triangle Pascalsches Dreieck
path Weg
pattern Muster, Modell, Vorlage
  checkerboard pattern Karomuster
Peano's Axioms Peano-Axiome
pedal curve Fußpunktskurve
pedal triangle Fußpunktdreieck
pencil of lines Strahlenbüschel, Geradenbüschel
pentagon Fünfeck, Pentagon
pentagonal number Fünfeckzahl, Pentagonalzahl
pentahedron Fünfflächner, Pentaeder
percent Prozent
percentage Prozentsatz, Prozentverhältnis
percentage calculation Prozentrechnung
perfect perfekt, fehlerlos, vollkommen
perfect cube vollständige dritte Potenz, vollständiger Kubus
perfect number vollkommene Zahl, perfekte Zahl

perfect square vollständiges Quadrat, Quadratzahl, Viereckzahl
perimeter Umfang, Rand
period Periode
periodic decimal fraction periodischer Dezimalbruch
permutation Permutation
  cyclic permutation zyklische Permutation
perpendicular senkrecht, lotrecht, normal, rechtwinklig
perpendicular bisector of line segment Streckensymmetrale
perpendicular lines normale Geraden, rechtwinklige Geraden
perpendicular plane Lotebene
place Stelle
place holder Platzhalter, Variable
place value Stellenwert
plane Ebene, eben, flach
plane trigonometry ebene Trigonometrie
Platonic solid Platonischer Körper (regelmäßiger) Körper
plot grafische Darstellung, (auf)zeichnen
plotter Drucker
plus sign Pluszeichen, positives Zeichen
point Punkt
  initial point Anfangspunkt
  singular point singulärer Punkt
  terminal point Endpunkt
point of discontinuity Unstetigkeitsstelle
point of inflection Wendepunkt
point of intersection Schnittpunkt
point (pole) of rotation Drehungspunkt, Drehpunkt
point-slope form of a linear equation Punktrichtungsgleichung der Geraden
polar axis Polarachse, Nullstrahl
polar circle Polarkreis
polar coordinates Polarkoordinaten
polar line Polare
polar point Pol
polar triangle Polardreieck
pole Pol, Polstelle
poll Umfrage
polygon Polygon, Vieleck
polygonal number Polygonalzahl, Vieleckszahl
polyhedron Vielflächner, Polyeder
polyhedron of *n* faces *n*-Flächner-, *n*-seitiges Polyeder
polynomial Polynom

population Population, Bevölkerung, Grundgesamtheit
positive positiv
postassessment Nachbeurteilung
potency Stärke, Macht, Mächtigkeit
power (as exponent) Potenz
power of a point with respect to a circle Potenz eines Punktes bezüglich eines Kreises
power series Potenzreihe
power set Potenzmenge
practical problem Sachrechnen
preassessment Voreinschätzung
preliminary einleitend, vorbereitend
preparatory vorbereitend
prevent verhindern
price Tarif, Preis
prime unteilbar, teilerfremd, prim
prime (mark) (') Strich (')
  a' *a prime* a Strich
  a'' *a double prime* a zwei Strich
prime factor Primfaktor
prime number Primzahl
prime pair Primzahlzwillinge
primitive root Primitivwurzel
primitive root of unit primitive Einheitswurzel
principal (financial) Grundkapital, Kapital
principal axis Hauptachse
principal axis transformation Hauptachsentransformation
principle of duality Dualitätsprinzip
prism Prisma
  right prism gerades Prisma
  oblique prism schiefes Prisma
  truncated prism abgeschnittenes Prisma
prismatic surface Prismenoberfläche
probability Wahrscheinlichkeit
  conditional probability bedingte Wahrscheinlichkeit
  theory of probability Wahrscheinlichkeitsrechnung
probability distribution Wahrscheinlichkeitsverteilung
problem Problem
  arithmetic problem arithmetische Aufgabe, Rechenaufgabe
problem solving Problemlösen
procedure Verfahren, Vorgehen
process of elimination Eliminationsverfahren

produce erzeugen
product Produkt
product rule Produktregel
profit Gewinn, Profit
profit and loss Gewinn and Verlust
progression Progression, Verlauf
  arithmetic progression arithmetische Progression
  continuous progression stetige Progression
  geometric progression geometrische Progression
projection Projektion
  skew projection Schrägriß, Schrägansicht
projective geometry projektive Geometrie
projective plane projektive Ebene
projectivity Projektivität
prolongation Fortsetzung, Verlängerung
proof Beweis
  direct proof direkter Beweis
  indirect proof indirekter Beweis
proof by mathematical induction Beweis durch vollständige Induktion
proof of existence Existenzbeweis
proper richtig, passend, echt
proper divisor echter Teiler
proper fraction echter Bruch
proper subset echte Untermenge
property Eigenschaft
proportion Proportion, Verhältnisgleichung
  direct direkte Proportion
  indirect indirekte Proportion
proportional proportional, verhältnisgleich
propose vorschlagen
proposition Vorschlag, Antrag, Satz
protractor Winkelmesser, Gradbogen
prove beweisen
Ptolemy's theorem Ptolemäischer Lehrsatz, Gegensehnensatz
pure rein
pure imaginary number rein imaginäre Zahl
pure quadratic equation rein quadratische Gleichung
purpose Zweck, Ziel, Absicht
pyramid Pyramide
  oblique pyramid schiefe Pyramide
  right pyramid gerade Pyramide
  square based pyramid quadratische Pyramide
  triangular pyramid dreiseitige Pyramide

Pythagorean theorem Pythagoreischer Lehrsatz
Pythagorean triple Pythagoreisches Zahlentripel

Q

quadrangle Viereck
quadrant Quadrant, Viertelebene
quadratic quadratisch
quadratic equation quadratische Gleichung
quadratic formula Lösungsformel für quadratische Gleichungen
quadratic residue quadratischer Rest
quadrilateral Viereck, Vierseit
  inscribed quadrilateral eingeschriebenes Viereck, Sehnenviereck
quantifier Quantifikator
quantity Quantität, Größe
quarter Viertel
quartile Quartil (Streuungsmaß)
quasi gleichsam, ähnlich
quinary notation quinäre Zahlendarstellung (Schreibweise) mit der Basis 5
quindecon Fünfzehneck, Quindekon
quotient Quotient
quotient field Quotientenkörper
quotient of differences Differenzenquotient
quotient rule Quotientenregel

R

radian Radiant (*Zeichen*: rad)
radian measure Bogenmaß
radical Wurzel, radikal
radical equation Wurzelgleichung
radical number Wurzelzahl
radical sign Wurzelzeichen
radical spiral Wurzelspirale
radius (*pl.* **radii**) Radius, Halbmesser (*pl.* Radien)
radius of convergence Konvergenzradius
radius of curvature Krümmungsradius
raise erheben
raise the price Warenpreis erhöhen
raising to a power Potenzieren, Erhebung zu einer Potenz

ramification Verzweigung
random zufällig
random error Zufallsfehler, statistischer Fehler
random event zufälliges Ereignis
random number Zufallszahl
random order zufällige Reihenfolge
random sample Zufallsauswahl, Stichprobe
random variable Zufallsvariable
range Zielbereich, Spannweite, Reichweite
range of a function Wertebereich einer Funktion
rank Rang
rank of a matrix Rang einer Matrix
rate Wechselkurs, Tarif, Prozentsatz
rate of growth Wachstumsgeschwindigkeit
rate of interest Zinssatz, Zinsrate
rate of speed Tempo, Geschwindigkeit
ratio Verhältnis
ratio of similitude Ähnlichkeitsverhältnis
ratio test Quotientenkriterium
rational fraction rationaler Bruch, kommensurabler Bruch
rational number rationale Zahl
rationalizing (denominator) rational machen (Nenner)
ray Strahl
real reell
real axis reelle Achse
real number reelle Zahl
real number system reelles Zahlensystem
real part Realteil
reality Realität
realize verwirklichen
rearrangement Umordnung (z. B. von Reihen)
reason ergründen, Grund, Vernunft
reason by induction induktiv schließen
recalculate nachrechnen
reciprocal value reziproker Wert, Kehrwert
reciprocal function reziproke Funktion
reciprocal ratio umgekehrtes Verhältnis
record Aufzeichnung, aufschreiben, protokollieren
recreation Unterhaltung, Erholung, Entspannung
rectangle Rechteck
rectangular rechteckig
recurrence Wiederkehr, Rekursion

recurring decimal periodische Dezimalzahl
recursion formula Rekursionsformel
recursive function rekursive Funktion
reduce verkleinern, reduzieren
reduce the fraction Bruch kürzen
reduced fraction gekürzter Bruch
refinement Veredelung, Feinheit, Verfeinerung
reflected image Spiegelbild
reflection in a line Achsenspiegelung
reflection in a plane Spiegelung an einer Ebene
reflexive reflexiv
region Bereich
regression Regression, Rückentwicklung
   linear regression lineare Regression
regular regelmäßig, regulär
regular polygon regelmäßiges Vieleck, reguläres Polygon
regular polyhedron regelmäßiger Vielflächner, reguläres Polyeder
regulation Vorschrift, Regelung
reinforce verstärken
reject verwerfen
relation Relation, Beziehung
   equivalence relation Äquivalenzrelation
   unary relation einstellige Relation
relative relativ
relative error relativer Fehler
relative frequency relative Häufigkeit
relative growth rate relative Wachstumsrate
relatively closed set relativ abgeschlossene Menge
relatively consistent relativ widerspruchsfrei
relatively prime teilerfremd
relatively prime numbers relativ prime Zahlen, teilerfremde Zahlen
reliability Zuverlässigkeit
remainder Rest (bei Division), Restbetrag
remote entfernt, abgelegen, gering
renumbering Umnumerierung
repeating decimal periodische Dezimalzahl
repetition Wiederholung
replacement Ersetzung, Zurücklegen, Rückerstattung
representation Darstellung
requirement Anforderung, Bedarf

research Forschung, wissenschaftliche Untersuchung
residual zurückbleibend, Rest ...
residue (class) Restklasse
residue theorem Residuensatz
respect Rücksicht
   with respect to hinsichtlich, bezüglich
respectively in dieser Reihenfolge
result Ergebnis
resultant of vectors Resultierende, Vektorsumme
retardation Verlangsamung
reversal of sign Vorzeichenwechsel, Vorzeichenänderung
reverse order in umgekehrter Reihenfolge
review Überprüfung, Rundschau, Rückschau, überprüfen, überblicken
revolution Drehung
   solid of revolution Drehkörper, Rotationskörper
rhombus Rhombus, Raute
right Recht, richtig, recht
right angle rechter Winkel
right-angled triangle *(Brit.)* rechtwinkliges Dreieck
right cone gerader Kegel
right cylinder gerader Zylinder
right distributativity rechtsseitige Distributivität
right distributive law rechtsseitiges Distributivgesetz
right hand parenthesis rechte Klammer
right identity element Rechtseinselement, rechtseitiges Einselement
right inverse rechtsinvers
right inverse element rechtsinverses Element
right prism gerades Prisma
right triangle *(Am.)* rechtwinkliges Dreieck
rigorous proof strenger Beweis
ring Ring
root Wurzel
   square root Quadratwurzel
root of unity Einheitswurzel
rotation Drehung
round rund, runden
round number gerundete Zahl
rounding down abrunden
rounding error Rundungsfehler
rounding off runden

rounding up aufrunden
row Reihe, Zeile, Spalte
rule Regel
rule for divisibility Teilbarkeitsregel
rule of thumb Faustregel, über den Daumen gepeilt
ruler Lineal

S

sample Musterbeispiel
sample (statistic) Stichprobe
sample mean Mittelwert der Stichprobe
sample size Stichprobenumfang
sample space Stichprobenraum
sample survey Stichprobenerhebung
sampling Stichprobennahme, Stichprobenentnahme, Stichprobenauswahl,
sampling error Stichprobenfehler
scalar Skalar, Zahl
scalar product Skalarprodukt
scalene triangle ungleichseitiges Dreieck
scatter diagram Punktwolke, Streubild, Streuungsdiagramm
schedule Zeitplan, Ordnung, Plan
scheme Schema
score Wertung
search suchen
secant (line) Sekante
secant (secant function) Sekans (Sekansfunktion)
second zweite(r)
secondly zweitens
section Schnitt, Abschnitt
  golden section Goldener Schnitt, stetige Teilung
sector Kreisausschnitt, Sektor
segment Abschnitt
  line segment Strecke
segment of a circle Kreissegment
semi axis Halbachse
semi-major axis große Halbachse
semi-minor axis kleine Halbachse
semicircle Halbkreis
semiperimeter halber Umfang
sense Sinn, Vernunft, fühlen, spüren
sentence Satz, Formel
separability Trennbarkeit, Separabilität
separate getrennt, trennen, zerlegen
sequence Folge, Sequenz
  arithmetic sequence atithmetische Folge
  bounded sequence beschränkte Folge
  convergent sequence konvergente Folge
  divergent sequence divergente Folge
  geometric sequence geometrische Folge
  harmonic sequence harmonische Folge
  unbounded sequence unbeschränkte Folge
sequence of numbers Zahlenfolge
sequence of points Punktfolge
sequence of prime numbers Primzahlenfolge
series Reihe
  arithmetic series arithmetische Reihe
  binomial series binomische Reihe
  geometric series geometrische Reihe
  harmonic series harmonische Reihe
series of numbers Zahlenreihe
set Menge
  closed set abgeschlossene Menge
  disjoint sets elementfremde (disjunkte) Mengen
  fundamental set Grundmenge
  null set leere Menge
  ordered set geordnete Menge
  unordered set ungeordnete Menge
  well ordered set wohlgeordnete Menge
set intersection Durchschnitt, Durchschnittsmenge
set of orderd pairs Menge geordneter Paare
set theory Mengenlehre, Mengentheorie
set union Vereinigung, Vereinigungsmenge
seven (seventh) sieben (siebente)
seventeen (seventeenth) siebzehn (siebzehnte)
seventeen sided polygon Siebzehneck, 17-Eck
seventh Siebentel
seventy (seventieth) siebzig (siebzigste)
sexagesimal arithmetic Sexagesimalarithmetik, Sexagesimalrechnung
sexagesimal system of notation Sexagesimalsystem
shape Gestalt, Form
share Anteil, Teil, teilen
sheet (of paper) Blatt (Papier)
shortage Mangel
shortest distance kürzester Abstand, kürzeste Strecke
side (of a polygon) Seite (eines Vielecks)

sign Zeichen
sign of implication (→) Impikationszeichen
sign of inclusion (⊂) Enthaltenszeichen
sign of intersection (∩) Zeichen der Durchschnittsbildung
sign of membership relation (∈) Zeichen der Elementbeziehung
sign of union (∪) Zeichen der Vereinigung
similar ähnlich
similarity Ähnlichkeit
simple fraction einfacher Bruch
simplification Vereinfachung
simplify vereinfachen
simplifying expressions Ausdrücke vereinfachen
simultaneous equations simultane Gleichungen, System von Gleichungen
sine (sine function) Sinus (Sinusfunktion)
singular matrix singuläre Matrix
singular point singulärer Punkt
six (sixth) sechs (sechste)
sixteen (sixteenth) sechzehn (sechzehnte)
sixth Sechstel
sixty (sixtieth) sechzig (sechzigste)
sketch Skizze, skizzieren
skew schräg, schief, asymmetrisch
skew lines windschiefe Geraden
skew projection Schrägriß, Schrägansicht
skewness Schiefe
skill Können, Sachkenntnis, Geschick
slant Schräge, schräg
slant height Seitenhöhe
slant height of a cone Mantellinie eines Kegels
slant height of a pyramid Seitenhöhe einer Pyramide
slide rule Rechenschieber, Rechenstab
slope Anstieg, Neigung, Steigung
solid Körper, Festkörper
solid geometry Geometrie in drei Dimensionen, Stereometrie, Geometrie der Körper
solid of equal volumes Körper mit gleichem Rauminhalt
solution Lösung
soluble lösbar, auflösbar
solvable lösbar
solve an equation Gleichung lösen
source Quelle
space Raum

spectrum Spektrum
sphere Kugel, Sphäre
spherical angle sphärischer Winkel, Kugelwinkel
spherical cap Kugelkalotte
spherical center sphärischer Mittelpunkt
spherical distance Kugelabstand
spherical excess sphärischer Exzeß
spherical geometry sphärische Geometrie, Kugelgeometrie
spherical lune Kugelzweieck
spherical segment of one base Kugelsegment
spherical segment of two bases Kugelschicht
spherical shell Kugelschale
spherical surface sphärische Fläche, Kugelfläche
spherical symmetry Kugelsymmetrie
spherical triangle sphärisches Dreieck, Kugeldreieck
spherical zone Kugelzone
spiral Spirale
square Quadrat, quadrieren
  magic square magisches Quadrat
square kilometer Quadratkilometer
square number Quadratzahl
square root Quadratwurzel
  to get square root of Quadratwurzelziehen
square unit Flächeneinheit
squaring the circle Quadratur des Kreises
standard deviation Standardabweichung, mittlere quadratische Abweichung
standard equation (equation in standard form) Gleichung in Normalform
statistical error zufälliger Fehler, statistischer Fehler
statistical inference symmetrische Verteilung
statistician Statistiker
statistics Statistik
step function Funktion mit Sprungstellen (Treppenfunktion)
straight gestreckt, gerade
straight angle gestreckter Winkel
straight line Gerade
straightedge Lineal
strength Stärke
strengthen stärken, verstärken

stretch Streckung, strecken
strive sich bemühen, streben
structure Struktur
   algebraic structure algebraische Struktur
subgroup Untergruppe
subscript tiefgestellte Zahl, unterer Index
subsequence Teilfolge
subset Untermenge, Teilmenge
   proper subset echte Untermenge
subspace Unterraum
substitution Substitution, Einsetzung
substitution formula Substitutionsregel
subtract subtrahieren, abziehen
subtraction Subtraktion,
subtrahend Subtrahend
successive (aufeinander)folgend
successor Nachfolger
suggestion Vorschlag
sum Summe
   lower sum Untersumme
   partial sum Partialsumme
   upper sum Obersumme
sum of the digits Ziffernsumme, Quersumme
summary Zusammenfassung
summation sign Summenzeichen (Σ)
superposition Überlagerung
superscript oberer Index, hochgestellte Zahl
supplement Ergänzung
supplementary angle Supplementwinkel
supplementary element ergänzendes Element
supplies Ausstattung, Ausrüstung
supply Bereitstellung, versorgen, bereitstellen
support unterstützen
surface Oberfläche
   lateral surface Seitenfläche (Mantelfläche)
surface area Oberflächeninhalt
surface integral Flächenintegral
surjective surjektiv
survey Erhebung, Überblick, überblicken, abschätzen
surveying Vermessung (Land)
symbolism Symbolik, symbolische Darstellung
symmetrical symmetrisch
symmetrical equation symmetrische Gleichung

symmetry Symmetrie
   axis of symmetry Symmetrieachse
   plane of symmetry Symmetrieebene
synthesize künstlich herstellen, zufügen
system System
   coordinate system Koordinatensystem
   decimal system Dezimalsystem
system of equations Gleichungssystem

T

t-distribution (Student's) t-Verteilung (Student-Verteilung)
table Tafel, Tabelle, Tisch
table of squares Quadrattafel
tail Schwanz
tally chart Strichliste
tan-chord angle Tangentensehnenwinkel
tangent (line) Tangente
tangent (tangent function) Tangens (Tangensfunktion)
tangent plane Tangentialebene
tangent vector Tangentenvektor
target Ziel, Zielscheibe
Taylor series Taylor-Reihe
ten (tenth) zehn (zehnte)
tendency Tendenz
tens digit Zehnerstelle
tension Spannung
tenth Zehntel
term Glied, Term
   like term gleichnamiger Term
terminal Grenz …, End …
terminal digit letzte Ziffer, Endziffer
tessellation Mosaikarbeit
test Prüfung, Versuch
tetrahedral angle Raumwinkel, aus drei Kanten gebildeter Winkel
theorem Lehrsatz
   binomial theorem binomischer Lehrsatz
   Pythagorean theorem pythagoräischer Lehrsatz
theorem of proportional segments Strahlensatz
theory of errors Fehlerrechnung
theory of numbers Zahlentheorie
theory of probability Wahrscheinlichkeitsrechnung
thesis Dissertation
third dritte(r), Drittel

thirteen (thirteenth) dreizehn (dreizehnte)
thirty (thirtieth) dreißig (dreißigste)
three drei
three times dreimal
threefold dreifach
tight knapp, dicht
tilt kippen, neigen
times (2 times 3) mal (2 mal 3)
tool Werkzeug, Gerät
top Spitze, höchste Stelle, Gipfel, oberer Teil
topic Thema, Abschnitt, Gesprächsgegenstand
topology Topologie
torus Torus, Ringkörper
trait Merkmal, Charakterzug
trajectory Bahnkurve
transcendental number transzendente Zahl
transfer Übertragung
transformation Umformung, Transformation
transitive transitiv
translation Schiebung
trapezoid *(Am.)*, **trapezium** *(Brit.)* Trapez
trial Versuch, Probe, Prüfung
triangle Dreieck
  acute triangle spitzwinkliges Dreieck
  equilateral triangle gleichseitiges Dreieck
  isosceles triangle gleichschenkliges Dreieck
  right triangle (Am.), right-angled triangle (Brit.) rechtwinkliges Dreieck
  scalene triangle ungleichseitiges Dreieck
triangle inequality Dreiecksungleichung
triangular dreieckig, dreiwinkelig
triangular matrix Dreiecksmatrix
triangular prism dreiseitiges Prisma
triangular pyramid dreiseitige Pyramide
trichotomy law Gesetz der Trichotomie
trigonometric functions trigonometrische Funktionen
trigonometry (plane, spherical) Trigonometrie (ebene, sphärische)
trihedral dreiflächig
trihedral angle Raumwinkel
trilateral dreiseitig
trinomial dreigliedrig
trisect in drei gleiche Teile teilen

trisection Dreiteilung
trisection of an angle Winkel-Dreiteilung
truncate abstumpfen, abschneiden
truncated cone (obliquely) abgeschnittener Kegel (schräg)
truncated cylinder (obliquely) abgeschnittener Zylinder (schräg)
truth table Wahrheitstafel
tube Röhre
tubular surface Röhrenfläche
turn Drehung, drehen
turn around umdrehen
twelfth Zwölftel
twelve (twelfth) zwölf (zwölfte)
twice zweimal
two zwei
two-digit integer zweistellige (zweiziffrige) ganze Zahl
type I (II) error Fehler 1. (2.) Art

U

unambiguous definition eindeutige Definition
unary relation einstellige Relation
unbiased erwartungstreu, unverfälscht
unbounded unbegrenzt, schrankenlos
unbounded interval unbeschränktes Intervall
unbounded set unbeschränkte Menge
uncertainty Ungewißheit, Unbestimmtheit
uncountable überabzählbar
undetermined unentschieden, unbestimmt
undetermined coefficient unbestimmter Koeffizient
undetermined number unbestimmte Zahl
undirected ungerichtet
undivided ungeteilt
unequal ungleich
uniform convergence gleichmäßige Konvergenz
uniform distribution gleichmäßige Verteilung, Gleichverteilung
union Vereinigung
union of sets Vereinigungsmenge
uniqueness Eindeutigkeit
unit Einheit
unit circle Einheitskreis
unit element Einselement
unit matrix Einheitsmatrix

unit of length Längeneinheit
unit of measurement Maßeinheit
unit square Einheitsquadrat
unit vector Einheitsvektor
unite vereinigen
unknown Unbekannte
unordered set ungeordnete Menge
unpredictable unvorhersehbar, unberechenbar
unsolvable unlösbare
upper ober, höher, Ober ...
upper bound obere Schranke
upper limit oberer Limes, obere Grenze
upper sum Obersumme
utility nützen, Nützlichkeit
utilize (be)nützen

V

valid gültig
valid formula gültige Formel
validate bestätigen, für gültig erklären
valuation Bewertung
value Wert
vanishing line Fluchtlinie, Fluchtgerade
vanishing point Fluchtpunkt
variable Variable
  auxiliary variable Hilfsvariable
  dependent variable abhängige Variable
  discrete variable diskrete Variable
  independent variable unabhängige Variable
  random variable Zufallsvariable
vector Vektor
vector addition Vektoraddition
vector algebra Vektoralgebra
vector calculations Vektorrechnung
vector decomposition Komponentenzerlegung eines Vektors
vector products Produkte von Vektoren
  inner (dot) product inneres Produkt (Skalarprodukt)
  outer (cross) product äußeres Produkt (Kreuzprodukt, vektorielles Produkt)
vector space Vektorraum
verify bestätigen
vertex (vertices) Scheitel, Spitze, Eckpunkt, Ecke
vertical angles Scheitelwinkel

vertical plane Vertikalebene
vertical row (column) Spalte, Kolonne, Vertikalreihe
Vieta's formulae Vietascher Wurzelsatz
void set (empty set) leere Menge, Nullmenge
volume Volumen, Rauminhalt
voluntary freiwillig

W

wave Welle
weakening Abschwächung
weakness Schwäche
weight Gewicht
weighted mean (average) gewichtetes Mittel
well-ordered set wohlgeordnete Menge
well defined eindeutig definiert, wohldefiniert
whole number ganze Zahl (im Gegensatz zum Bruch)
width Breite, Weite
withdrawal Rücknahme, Bankguthaben auflösen, Widerrufung

X

x-axis x-Achse
x,y coordinates x,y Koordinaten
xy-plane xy-Ebene

Y

y-axis y-Achse
yield hervorbringen (Ertrag)

Z

zenith Scheitelpunkt, Zenit
zero Null
zero divisor Nullteiler
zero element Nullelement
zero of a polynomial Nullstelle eines Polynoms

2. Teil
Deutsch–Englisch

A

Abbildung mapping, map
Abgaben (Steuerabgaben) deduction (tax deduction)
abgeschlossen closed
abgeschlossen bezüglich einer Verknüpfung closed with respect to an operation
abgeschlossene Abbildung closed mapping
abgeschlossene Menge closed set
abhängig dependent
Abhängigkeit dependence
ableitbar deducible, derivable
ableiten derive, deduce, differentiate
Ableitung (Differentialquotient) derivative
  äußere Ableitung outer derivative
  innere Ableitung inner derivative
  partielle Ableitung partial derivative
Ableitung erster Ordnung first order derivative
Ableitungsregel differentiation rule
abmessen measure
abrunden rounding down
abschätzen estimate
Abschätzung estimation
abschlagen (Strecke) mark-off
Abschnitt segment, section
Abschnitt auf der x-Achse x-intercept
abschreiben copy
Abschwächung weakening
Absolutbetrag absolute value
absolute Häufigkeit absolute frequency
absolute Klassenhäufigkeit absolute cell (class) frequency
absoluter Fehler absolute error
Absolutwert absolute value
Abstand distance
abstumpfen (abschneiden) truncate
Abszisse abscissa
Abweichung deviation, deflection, variation
  Standardabweichung standard deviation
Abweichung vom Mittelwert deviation from the mean
abzählbar countable
Abzählbarkeit countability
Abzählbarkeitsaxiom axiom of countability
abzählen count
abziehen subtract, deduct
Achse (x-Achse) axis (x-axis)
  große Achse major axis
  imaginäre Achse imaginary axis
  kleine Achse minor axis
  reelle Achse real axis
Achsenspiegelung line reflection, reflection in a line
Achsensymmetrie axial symmetry, mirror symmetry
acht (achte) eight (eighth)
Achteck octagon
Achtel eighth
Achtflächner (Oktaeder) octahedron
achtzehn (achtzehnte) eighteen (eighteenth)
achtzig (achtzigste) eighty (eightieth)
addieren add
Addition addition
Additionstabelle addition table
Additionszeichen addition sign, plus sign
adjungierte Abbildung adjoint mapping
adjungierte Matrix adjoint matrix
affin affine
affine Abbildung affine map
affiner Raum affine space
Affinität affinity
ähnlich similar
Ähnlichkeit similarity
Ähnlichkeitsverhältnis ratio of similitude
Algebra algebra
algebraisch abgeschlossen algebraically closed
algebraische Gleichung algebraic equation
algebraische Körpererweiterung algebraic field extension
algebraische Struktur algebraic structure
algebraische Zahl algebraic number
Algorithmus algorithm
alternierend alternating
alternierende Gruppe alternating group

Amplitude amplitude
Analogrechner analog computer
analysieren (genau untersuchen) analyze
Analysis analysis, calculus
analytische Funktion analytic function
analytische Geometrie analytic geometry
aneignen (sich) acquire
anfänglich initial
Anfangsglied first term
Anfangspunkt initial point, origin (point)
Anforderung requirement
anführendes Glied leading term
angrenzend adjacent
Ankathete adjacent side
Ankreis (angeschriebener Kreis) excircle (escribed circle)
annähernd approximate
Annahme acceptance, assumption
annehmbar acceptable
annehmen accept, assume
anordnen arrange, order
Anordnung (Permutation) arrangement (permutation)
Anordnung der Größe nach arrangement according to magnitude
Anordnung nach aufsteigenden (absteigenden) Potenzen arrangement in ascending (descending) powers
Anstieg ascent, rise
Antithese antithesis
Antrag application, motion
Anweisung instruction, assignment
anwenden apply, use
Anwendung application, use
Anwendungsbeispiel application example, application problem
anwendungsorientiert application-oriented
Anzahl number
Approximation (Näherung) approximation
Approximationsfehler error of approximation
Äquivalenz equivalence
Äquivalenzbeziehung equivalence relation
Äquivalenzklasse equivalence class
Äquivalenzrelation equivalence relation
Arbeit work
Arbeitsablauf process of work
Arbeitsblatt work sheet, activity sheet

Arcusfunktion inverse trigonometric function
Argument argument
argumentieren argue
Arithmetik arithmetic
arithmetische Aufgabe arithmetic problem
arithmetische Folge arithmetic sequence
arithmetische Progression arithmetic progression
arithmetisches Mittel arithmetic mean (average)
Arkusfunktion arc function
Arkuskosekans arc cosecant
Arkuskosinus arc cosine
Arkuskotangens arc cotangent
Arkussekans arc secant
Arkussinus arc sine
Arkustangens arc tangent
assoziativ associative
assoziative binäre (zweistellige) Operation associative binary operation
assoziativer kommutativer Ring associative commutative ring
Assoziativgesetz associative law
Assoziativität associativity
assoziieren associate
Astroide asteroid
Asymptote asymptote
aufeinanderfolgend successive
Aufgabe exercise, task, assignment
Aufgabe zuweisen assign
auflösbar solvable, soluble
auflösen nach solve for
Auflösungsformel für quadratische Gleichungen quadratic formula
Aufmerksamkeit attention
Aufriß elevation, vertical projection
aufrunden rounding up
aufschlagen (Warenpreis) go up, raise (in price)
aufschreiben write down
aufsteigende Anordnung (aufsteigend geordnet) ascending order
aufsteigende (steigende, wachsende) Potenzen ascending powers
aufsteigender Kettenbruch ascending continued fraction
aufstellen (Tabelle) construct (a table)
Aufstellung array, table, list, formation, tabulation, arrangement, itemization

auftauchen (erscheinen)   emerge, come up, turn up
aufteilen   divide (up), split (up), divide
aufzeichnen   draw, sketch, write down, record
Ausdehnung   extension, expansion, stretch
Ausdruck   term, expression
Ausdrücke vereinfachen   simplifying expressions
ausdrücken   express
Ausgabe   issue, output
ausklammern   factor out
ausradieren (löschen)   erase
ausrechnen   calculate, work out
Ausrüstung   equipment, supplies
Aussage   statement, proposition
Aussageform   open sentence
Ausstattung   equipment, supplies
ausstellen   write out, exhibit
ausstreichen   delete, cancel
Auswahlaxiom   axiom of choice
ausweichen (vermeiden)   avoid
auswendiglernen   memorize
auswerten   evaluate, interpret
Auswertung   evaluation
außen   external
außenberührend   externally tangent
Außenglied   extreme term of a proportion
Außenwinkel   exterior angle
äußere Ableitung   outer derivative
äußerer Punkt   exterior point
Äußeres   exterior, outer
Authentizität (Echtheit)   authenticity
Automorphismus   automorphism
Axiom   axiom

B

Bahnkurve   trajectory
Balkendiagramm   bar graph
Basis   base, basis
Basisvektor   basis vector
Baumdiagramm   tree diagram
Bausteinprinzip   building block principle
bedeutend   important, significant, outstanding
bedingt konvergent   conditionally convergent
bedingte Wahrscheinlichkeit   conditional probability
Bedingung   condition
Bedürfnis (nach)   need (for), requirement
Befähigung   ability, talent, qualification
begabt   gifted
begleiten   accompany
begreifen   understand, comprehend
Begrenzung   boundary, limit
Begriff   concept, term, expression
Begründung   reason, justification, explanation
begünstigen   foster
Behauptung   assertion, claim
Beherrschung   mastery
Beispiel (zum Beispiel)   example (for example, for instance)
beisteuern (beitragen)   contribute
belegen   overlay
beliebig (groß/klein)   arbitrarily (large/small)
benachbart   neighboring, adjacent
benützen   use, utilize
Beobachtung   observation
Beobachtungsfehler   error of observation
berechnen   calculate, compute, evaluate
Berechnung   calculation, computation, evaluation
Bereich   area, region, field
Bereich (algebraischer)   domain
Bereicherung   enrichment
Bernoulli-Verteilung   Bernoulli distribution
Berührung   contact, touch, contiguity
Berührung von innen   internal tangency
Berührungspunkt   point of tangency
beschäftigen   employ, occupy
Beschleunigung   acceleration
beschränkt   bounded
beschränkte Folge   bounded sequence
 nach oben beschränkte Folge   bounded sequence from above
 nach unten beschränkte Folge   bounded sequence from below
beschreibende Statistik   descriptive statistics
beschriften   label
Besserung   improvement
Bestandsaufnahme   inventory
bestätigen   verify, validate, confirm
betonen   accentuate, mention
Betrag (einer Rechnung)   amount
Betrag (einer Zahl)   value
 Absolutbetrag   absolute value
Beurteilung   evaluation, assessment, judgment

Bevölkerung population
Bewegung movement, motion
Beweis proof
   direkter Beweis direct proof
   indirekter Beweis indirect proof
Beweis durch vollständige Induktion proof by mathematical induction
beweisbar provable
beweisen prove
Bewertung evaluation
bewußt conscious, aware
Bezeichnung designation
bijektiv bijective
bilinear bilinear
Billion (10^{12}) trillion *(Am.)*, billion *(Brit.)*
Binärsystem binary number system
Binomialentwicklung binomial expansion
Binomialverteilung binomial distribution
binomische Reihe binomial series
Binomischer Lehrsatz binomial theorem
Blatt (Papier) sheet (of paper)
Bogen arc
   eingeschlossener Bogen intercepted arc
Bogenlänge length of an arc
Bogenmaß radian measure
Boolesche Algebra Boolean Algebra
Breite width
Brennpunkt focus
Brennpunktabstand focal distance
Brennstrahl focal radius
Bruch fraction
   echter Bruch proper fraction
   gleichnamige Brüche fractions with a common denominator
   unechter Bruch improper fraction
   uneigentlicher Bruch improper fraction
Bruch kürzen reduce the fraction to lowest terms
Bruch mit gleichem Nenner fraction with equal denominator
Bruchgleichung fractional equation
Bruchrechnung calculation with fractions
Bruchstrich fraction bar
Bruttoeinkommen gross earnings

C

Cauchy-Riemannsche Differentialgleichungen Cauchy-Riemann equations

Charakter character
Charakteristik characteristic
Chi-Quadrat-Test Chi-square test
Chi-Quadrat-Verteilung Chi-square distribution
Chinesischer Restsatz Chinese remainder theorem
Computer computer
Computerausdruck computer printout
Computergrafik computer graphics
Computerspiel computer game
computerunterstützter Unterricht computer-assisted instruction
Computerwissenschaft computer science

D

Damebrett checkerboard, chessboard
Darstellung representation
Datei file
Daten data
Dedekindscher Schnitt Dedekind cut
deduktiv deductive
deduktiv schließen reason by deduction
definieren define
Definition definition
Definitionsbereich domain
Definitionsbereich einer Funktion domain of a function
Dekade decade
Dekaeder (Zehnflächner) decahedron
Dekagon (Zehneck) decagon
Deltoid kite
Determinante (n-ter Ordnung) determinant (of the n-th order)
Dezimal ... decimal
Dezimalbruch decimal fraction
Dezimalbruchentwicklung decimal expansion
Dezimalpunkt decimal point
Dezimalstelle decimal place
Dezimalsystem decimal system
Dezimalzahl decimal number
Diagonale diagonal
Diagonalenschnittpunkt point of intersection of the diagonals
Diagramm (Graph) graph
Dichte density
Didaktik didactics
Differential differential

Differentialquotient derivative
Differential- und Integralrechnung differential and integral calculus
Differentiation differentiation
Differentiationsregeln derivative formulas
Differenz difference
Differenzenquotient quotient of differences
Differenzenverfahren method of finite-differences
Differenzierbarkeit differentiability
differenzieren differentiate
Digitalrechner digital computer
Diophantische Gleichung Diophantine equation
direkt direct
disjunkte (elementfremde) Mengen disjoint sets
Diskont (Satz) discount (rate)
diskret discrete
diskrete Zufallsvariable discontinuous variable (discrete)
Diskriminante discriminant
Dissertation thesis
Distanz (Entfernung, Abstand) distance
Distributivgesetz distributive law
divergent divergent
Divergenz divergence
Dividend dividend
dividieren (durch) divide (by)
Division (Teilung) division
Divison mit Rest division with remainder
Divisionszeichen division sign
Divisor (Teiler) divisor
Dodekaeder (Zwölfflächner) dodecahedron
Dodekagon (Zwölfeck) dodecagon
Doppelkegel double cone
doppelt double
doppelt logarithmisches Papier (Potenzpapier) log-log paper
Drachenviereck kite
Drehkegel cone of revolution
Drehkörper (Rotationskörper) solid of revolution
Drehung rotation, revolution, turn
Drehungspunkt (Drehpunkt) point (or pole) of rotation
drei (dritte) three (third)
Dreieck triangle

gleichseitiges Dreieck equilateral triangle
gleichschenkliges Dreieck isosceles triangle
rechtwinkliges Dreieck right (-angled) triangle
spitzwinkliges Dreieck acute triangle
stumpfwinkliges Dreieck obtuse triangle
ungleichseitiges Dreieck scalene triangle
dreieckig (dreiwinklig) triangular
Dreiecksmatrix triangular matrix
Dreiecksungleichung triangle inequality
dreifach threefold
dreiflächig trihedral
dreigliedrig trinomial
dreimal three times
dreiseitig trilateral
dreißig (dreißigste) thirty (thirtieth)
Dreiteilung trisection
dreizehn (dreizehnte) thirteen (thirteenth)
Drittel third
drittens thirdly
Dualitätsprinzip principle of duality
durch denselben Punkt gehend concurrent
Durchführung realization
Durchmesser diameter
Durchschnitt (Mittel) average
Durchschnittsmenge set intersection

E

eben level, plane
Ebene plane
ebene Trigonometrie plane trigonometry
echt proper
echte Teilmenge (Untermenge) proper subset
echter Bruch proper fraction
echter Teiler proper divisor
Ecke vertex, corner
Eckenanzahl number of vertices
eckig angular
Eckpunkt vertex, (*pl.* vertices)
Effizienz efficiency
eiförmig egg-shaped, ovoid
Eigenschaft property, characteristic
Eigenwert eigenvalue
Eilinie oval

eindeutig unique
eindeutig definiert well-defined
eindeutige Definition unambiguous definition
Eindeutigkeit uniqueness
eindimensional one dimensional
eine Parallele ziehen zu draw a parallel to
eineindeutige Abbildung one-to-one mapping
eineinhalb one and one-half
Einer one-digit number, unit
Einerziffer unit's digit
einfach simple
einfacher Bruch simple fraction
Einfachsprung single jump
Einfallswinkel angle of incidence
einfügen insert
einführen establish, insert, introduce
Eingabe input
Einheit unit, unity
Einheitselement identity element
Einheitskreis unit circle
Einheitsmatrix identity matrix
Einheitsquadrat unit square
Einheitsstrecke unit of length
Einheitsvektor unit vector
Einheitswurzel root of unity
Einhüllende envelope
einhundert one hundred
einigermaßen gut moderately good, fair
einklammern put in parentheses
Einkommen earnings, income
Einkommensteuer income tax
einleitend (vorbereitend) preliminary
einmal once
Einmaleins multiplication tables
einpassen adjust, fit in
einrechnen take into account
eins one
  die Eins the numeral one
Einsatz insertion
einschalten (von Zwischenwerten) interpolate
einschätzen estimate, assess
Einschätzung estimation, assessment
einschließen include
einschränken restrict
einschreiben inscribe
einseitig one sided, unilateral
Einselement unit element
einsetzen substitute, insert

Einsetzung substitution
einstellig one-digit
einstellige Relation unary relation
eintausend one thousand
eintreten enter, occur
einwertig single-valued
Einzahl singular
einzeichnen draw in, fill in, sketch, plot
Einzelfall individual case
einzeln single
Einzigkeitsprinzip uniqueness principle
elastisch elastic
Element element
elementfremde Mengen disjoint sets
Elevationswinkel angle of elevation
elf (elfte) eleven (eleventh)
Elftel eleventh
Eliminationsverfahren process of elimination
Eliminierung elimination
Elle cubit
Ellipse ellipse
elliptisch elliptical
Empfindlichkeit sensitivity
empirisch empirical
empirische Erwartung empirical expectation
empirische Varianz empirical variance
Endglied last term
endgültig conclusive, definitive, final
endlich finally, limited, finite, terminating
endliche Grundgesamtheit finite population
endliche Reihe finite series
endlos endless, infinite
Endpunkt end point
Endwert final value, accumulated result
Endziffer last digit
eng tight, narrow, restricted
entartet (degeneriert) degenerate
entbehrlich dispensable
entfernt remote, distant, far away
Entfernung distance, removal
entgegengesetzt opposite
entgegengesetzt zum Uhrzeigersinn counterclockwise
entgegengesetzte Vorzeichen opposite signs
entgegengesetzter Vektor opposite vector
entgegengesetztes Ereignis complementary event

Enthaltenszeichen ($\subset$) sign of inclusion
Entscheidung decision
entsprechend corresponding, appropriate
entwerfen design, sketch, draft
entwickeln generate, develop
Entwicklung development, expansion
Entwurf design
entziffern decipher, decode
Erdbahn earth's orbit
Ereignis event
Erfahrung experience
erfinderisch inventive
Erfindung invention
Erfolg success
erforschen explore, investigate
ergänzen supplement, complete
ergänzendes Element supplementary element
Ergänzung supplementation, completion
Ergebnis result, outcome, answer
ergründen reason, to find out, probe into, investigate
erhabener Winkel (überstumpf) reflex angle
erhältlich available
erheben raise
Erhebung survey, elevation
Erhebung zu einer Potenz raising to a power
Erhöhung increase
erlangen (Wissen) acquire
erraten guess
erreichbar attainable
erreichbare Genauigkeit attainable accuracy
erreichen attain, reach
ersetzen replace, substitute
Ersetzung substitution
erst first
erstens firstly
erwarten anticipate, expect, wait for
Erwartung expectation
erwartungstreu unbiased
erweitern extend, improve (Kenntnisse), augment (vergrößern)
erweiterte Matrix augmented matrix
erwünscht desirable, welcome
erzeugen produce, generate, create
erzeugende Funktion generating function
Euklidische Geometrie Euclidean geometry
Euklidischer Algorithmus Euclidean division algorithm
Eulersche Gerade Euler line
Eulersche Zahl Euler number
ewig eternal, perpetual, forever
exemplarisch exemplary
Existenzbeweis proof of existence
Exponent exponent
Exponentialfunktion exponential function
Exponentialverteilung exponential distribution
Extremum mit Nebenbedingungen extremum with auxiliary conditions
Extremwert extremum
Extremwertaufgabe extreme value problem
Exzentrizität eccentricity
Exzeß (sphärischer) excess (spherical)

F

***F*-Test** *F*-test
***F*-Verteilung** *F*-distribution, variance ratio distribution
Faden thread, string
Fähigkeit (Befähigung) ability
Faktor factor
  größter gemeinsamer Faktor greatest common factor
Faktorielle factorial
Fakultät factorial, faculty
Fall case, fall
fallen (abnehmen) decrease, descend, drop
fallende Anordnung descending order
fallende Progression decreasing progression
falsch false
falten fold
Faltung convolution, fold
Familie family
Faser fiber
fassen hold, grab, take
fast almost, nearly
Faustregel, „über den Daumen gepeilt" rule of thumb
Fehlen (Mangel) deficiency, absence, lack
fehlen (vermißt werden) to be missing
fehlender Wert missing value
Fehler error, mistake, fault
Fehlerabschätzung error approximation

Fehleranalyse　error analysis
Fehlerrechnung　calculus of errors
Feinheit　refinement
Feld　field
Festkommadarstellung　fixed point representation
Festkörper　solid
Festsetzung　postulation
Fibonacci Folge　Fibonacci sequence
Figur　figure
Fläche　area, surface, face (of a solid)
Flächenanteil　surface region portion
Flächeneinheit　square unit
flächengleich　equal in area
Flächeninhalt　area
Flächenintegral　surface integral
Flächenmaß　area measure
Flächenwinkel　dihedral angle
Fluchtlinie (Fluchtgerade)　vanishing line
Fluchtpunkt　vanishing point
Flugbahn　trajectory
Fokus　focus
Fokusweite　focal length
Folge　sequence
　arithmetische Folge　arithmetic sequence
　geometrische Folge　geometric sequence
　harmonische Folge　harmonic sequence
Folgerichtigkeit　logical order
folgern　deduce, infer
Folgerung　conclusion, implication
Folgesatz　corollary
fördern　foster
Form　form, shape
Formel (gültige)　formula (valid)
Forschung　research
Fortsetzung　prolongation, continuation
Freiheitsgrade　degrees of freedom
freiwillig　voluntary
fremd　disjoint, extraneous, strange
früher　previous
Fundamentalgruppe　fundamental group
Fundamentalsatz der Algebra　Fundamental Theorem of Algebra
Fundamentalsatz der Differential- und Integralrechnung　Fundamental Theorem of Calculus
fünf (fünfte)　five (fifth)
Fünfeck　pentagon
Fünfeckzahl　pentagonal number
Fünfflächner　pentahedron
fünfmal　five times

Fünfstern　pentagram
Fünftel　fifth
fünfzehn (fünfzehnte)　fifteen (fifteenth)
Fünfzehneck　quindecon
fünfzig (fünfzigst)　fifty (fiftieth)
Funktion　function
　Definitionsbereich einer Funktion　domain of a function
　ganze Funktion　entire function
　gerade Funktion　function of even degree
　konstante Funktion　constant function
　rekursive Funktion　recursive function
　reziproke Funktion　reciprocal function
　stetige Funktion　continuous function
　Wertebereich einer Funktion　range of a function
Funktion in einer Variablen　function of one variable
Funktion mit Sprungstellen (Treppenfunktion)　step function
funktional　functional
funktionale Abhängigkeit　functional dependence
Funktionenkörper　field of a function
Funktionsgraph　graph of a function
Funktionsterm　term of a function
Funktionswert　function value
für gültig erklären　validate
Fuß　foot
Fußpunkt des Lotes　foot of a perpendicular
Fußpunktdreieck　pedal triangle
Fußpunktkurve　pedal curve

G

Galois Theorie　Galois theory
ganze Funktion　entire function
ganze Zahl　whole number, integer
ganzrationale Funktion　polygonal function
ganzzahlig　integral
Gauß-Verteilung　normal distribution
Gaußsches Eliminationsverfahren　Gaussian elimination
Gebiet　domain (Bereich), area (Fläche), region, district (Gegend)
gebogen　bent, curved
Gebrauch　application
gebrochen　broken, fractional

gebunden bound
Gedächtnis memory
geeignet appropriate, suitable
Gefälle slope, gradient
gegeben given
Gegenbeispiel counterexample
Gegend neighborhood, region, surroundings
Gegendrehung counterrotation
Gegengewicht counterbalance
Gegenimplikation converse implication
Gegenkathete opposite leg (of a right triangle)
Gegenkraft counterforce, reaction
Gegenkrümmung reverse curvature
Gegensatz contrast
Gegensehnensatz Ptolemy's theorem on the inscribed quadrilateral
gegenseitig mutual
Gegensinn opposite sense
Gegenstand object, topic
Gegenteil contrary, opposite
gegenüberliegend opposite
gegenüberliegende Kante opposite edge
gegenüberliegender Eckpunkt opposite vertex
gegenüberliegender Winkel opposite angle
Gegenuhrzeigerrichtung counterclockwise
Gegenwert equivalent
Gegenwirkung reaction
Gehalt content(s), capacity, salary
gekrümmt curved
gekürzter Bruch reduced fraction, fraction in lowest terms
Gelenk joint, link
Gelenkkette series of links, linkage
gelten hold true, to be worth
Geltung validity
gemein common, ordinary
gemeinsam common, joint
gemeinsame Tangenten common tangents
gemeinsamer Nenner common denominator
gemeinsamer Teiler common factor
gemischte Zahl mixed number
genau exact, precise, accurate, true
„genau dann, wenn" (↔) "if and only if", biconditional
Geometrie geometry

Geometrie der Körper solid geometry
geometrische Folge geometric sequence
geometrische Progression geometric progression
geometrische Reihe geometric series
geometrische Verteilung geometric distribution
geometrischer Ort locus (geometric)
geometrisches Mittel geometric mean (average)
geordnetes Paar ordered pair
Gerade line, straight line
  ausgezogene Gerade solid line
  punktierte Gerade dotted line
  strichlierte Gerade dashed line
gerade (Zahl) even (number), straight
gerade Funktion even function
Geradenbüschel pencil of lines
Geradengleichung equation of a straight line
gerader Kegel right cone
gerader Zylinder right cylinder
Gerät equipment (Ausrüstung), tool (Werkzeug), apparatus, instrument
gerecht fair, just
gerichtete Strecke directed line segment
gerundete Zahl round number
Gerüst framework, frame, scaffolding
Gesamtwert total value
Geschick skill, aptitude
geschickt skillful
Geschwindigkeit speed, velocity
Geschwindigkeitsänderung change in velocity or speed
Gesetz law
Gesetz der Logik law of logic
Gesetz großer Zahlen law of large numbers
Gestalt (Form) shape
gestreckt (gerade) straight
gestreckter Winkel straight angle
Gewicht weight
Gewichtssatz set of weights
Gewinn profit
gewöhnen get used (or accustomed)
gewöhnliche Differntialgleichung ordinary differential equation
Gitter lattice
Gitterpunkt lattice point
Glaubwürdigkeit authenticity
gleich the same, equal, like

gleiche Potenz (Glied) like power
gleiche Winkel equal angles
Gleichgewicht balance
Gleichheit parity, equality
gleichmächtig equivalent
gleichmäßige Konvergenz uniform convergence
gleichmäßige Verteilung uniform distribution
gleichnamige Operation like operation
gleichnamiger Term like term
gleichschenkelig isosceles
gleichseitig equilateral
gleichsetzen equate
Gleichsetzungsverfahren elimination by comparison
Gleichung equation
Gleichung der Geraden (Punkt-Richtungsform) linear equation (point-slope form)
Gleichung dritten Grades cubic equation
Gleichung fünften Grades quintic equation
Gleichung in Normalform equation in standard form
Gleichung in Parameterdarstellung parametric equation
Gleichung in zwei Variablen equation with two variables
Gleichung lösen solve an equation
Gleichung n-ten Grades equation of n-th degree
Gleichung vierten Grades quartic equation
Gleichungssystem system of equations
Gleichverteilung uniform distribution
Gleichwertigkeit equivalence
gleichwinklig equiangular
Gleitkommadarstellung floating decimal point representation
Glied term
  erstes Glied first term
  letztes Glied last term
Glied mit der höchsten Potenz leading term
Gliederung grouping
Glockenkurve bell-shaped curve
Grad (Ordnung) degree (order)
Gradbogen protractor
grafische Darstellung graphic representation, chart

grafische Lösung graphic solution
grafisches Papier graph paper
Graph graph
Grenz ... terminal
Grenze boundary
Grenzwert limit
  oberer Grenzwert upper limit
  unterer Grenzwert lower limit
Grenzwertsätze limit theorems
Grenzzahl limit number
Grenzzeichen limit symbol (lim)
grob rough, coarse
grober Schnitzer howler
Größe size, quantity
Größenbestimmung magnitude determination
Größenordnung order of magnitude
Größenverhältnis proportion, ratio
größer als (>) greater than
Großkreis great circle
Großkreisbogen great circle arc
größter gemeinsamer Faktor greatest common factor
größter gemeinsamer Teiler greatest common divisor
Grund reason, basis, foundation, ground
Grundbegriff fundamental concept
Grundfläche base, bottom
Grundgesetz basic law
Grundintegral fundamental integral
Grundkapital principal (financial)
Grundkonstruktion basic construction
Grundkreis base circle, circle of inversion
Grundlage foundation
Grundlinie base line
Grundmaß fundamental unit
Grundmenge fundamental set
Grundrechnungsart arithmetical operation
Grundsatz axiom, postulate, principle
Grundriß horizontal projection
Grundvektor basis vector
Grundwert base
Grundzahl cardinal number, base of a power
Gruppe group
Gruppe bezüglich der Addition group with respect to addition
Gruppenbildung grouping
Gruppeneigenschaft group property
Gruppenelement group element

Gruppentheorie group theory
gruppieren group
Gruppierung grouping
gültig valid
  für gültig erklären validate
gültige Formel valid formula
günstig favorable
günstiges Ereignis favorable event
Gürtel girdle, ring, belt, zone of a sphere

H

halb half
Halbachse semi axis
  große Halbachse semi-major axis
  kleine Halbachse semi-minor axis
Halbebene half plane
halber Umfang semiperimeter
Halbgruppe semigroup
halbieren bisect
Halbierende bisector
Halbierung bisection
Halbierungslinie bisector (line)
Halbierungspunkt midpoint
Halbkreis semicircle
halbkreisförmig semicircular
Halbkugel hemisphere
Halblinie ray, half-line
Halbmesser radius
Halbordnung partial ordering
Halbraum half space
Halbwinkel half angle
harmonisch harmonic
harmonische Folge harmonic sequence
harmonisches Mittel harmonic mean
Haufen heap, cluster, pile
häufig frequent
Häufigkeit frequency
Häufigkeitskurve frequency curve
Häufigkeitstabelle frequency table
Häufigkeitsverteilung frequency distribution
Häufungspunkt accumulation point, cluster point
Häufungswert limiting value
Hauptachse principal axis, major axis
Hauptachsentransformation principal axis transformation
Hauptdiagonale leading diagonal
Hauptnenner least common denominator

Hauptpunkt principal point
Hebel lever
heben raise
herangehen (nähern) approach
herausfallen fall out, drop out, cancel out
herausfordern challenge
Herausforderung challenge
Herstellung production
herumdrehen turn around, rotate about
herunterfallen fall down
hervorbringen (Ertrag) yield
Herzkurve cardioid
heterogen heterogeneous
Heuler howler
Heuristik heuristic
Hexaeder (Sechsflächner) hexahedron
Hilfskonstruktion auxiliary construction
Hilfslinie auxiliary line
Hilfssatz auxilliary theorem, lemma
Hilfsvariable auxiliary variable
Hinlänglichkeit sufficiency
Hinlänglichkeitsbeweis proof of sufficiency
hinreichend sufficient
hinreichende Bedingung sufficient condition
hinsichtlich with respect to
hinten back, behind, rear
hinter behind
hinüber across, over
hinunter down(ward)
Hinweis hint
hinzufügen add
Histogramm histogram
hoch high
hochgestellte Zahl superscript
Hochpunkt maximum point
höchst maximum, highest
höchster Koeffizient leading coefficient
Höchstwert maximum value
Hochzahl (Exponent) exponent
Hoffnung expectation, hope
Höhe altitude, height
Höhe der Seitenfläche einer Pyramide slant height of pyramid
Höhe der Summe amount
Höhenschnittpunkt orthocenter
Höhle concavity, hollow
homogen homogeneous
homogenes Gleichungssystem homogeneous equation system

Homomorphismus homomorphism
Horizont horizon
horizontal horizontal
Horner-Schema Horner's method
hundert (hundertste) hundred (hundredth)
Hundertsatz (Prozentsatz) percentage
Hundertstel hundredth
Hyperbel hyperbola
Hyperbelast branch of hyperbola
Hyperbelfunktion hyperbolic function
hyperbolisch hyperbolic
hyperbolische Geometrie hyperbolic geometry (Lobachevskian)
Hypotenuse hypotenuse
Hypothese (Nullhypothese) hypothesis (null hypothesis)

I

identische Gleichheit identity
Identität identity
Ikosaeder (Zwanzigflächner) icosahedro
imaginär imaginary
imaginäre Achse imaginary axis
imaginäre Wurzel imaginary root
imaginäre Zahl imaginary number
Imaginärteil imaginary part
Implikation implication, conditional statement
Implikationszeichen ($\rightarrow$) sign of implication
implizieren imply
implizit implicit
Index (hochgestellter/tiefgestellter) superscript, subscript
Indexmenge index set
indirekt proportional inverse proportional
indirekter Beweis indirect proof
Induktion induction
induktiv schließen reason by induction
Informatik computer science
Informatiker computer scientist
Informationsverlust loss of information
Inhalt contents (Buch), capacity, volume (Rauminhalt)
injektiv injective
inkommensurabel incommensurable
Inkreis inscribed circle, incircle
Inkreismittelpunkt incenter *(Am.)*, incentre *(Brit.)*

Inkreisradius inradius, radius of inscribed circle
innen inside, internal
Innenwinkel interior angle
inner inner, inside, interior, internal, intrinsic
 innere Ableitung inner derivative
 inneres Produkt (Skalarprodukt) inner product (dot product)
Inneres interior
innerhalb inside, within
innerlich innate, intrinsic
Integral integral
 bestimmtes Integral definite integral
 unbestimmtes Integral indefinite integral
 uneigentliches Integral improper integral
Integralrechnung integral calculus
Integration integration
Integrationsmethode integration technique
integrierbar integrable
integrieren integrate
Integritätsbereich integral domain
Interpolation interpolation
Intervall interval
 abgeschlossenes Intervall closed interval
 offenes Intervall open interval
Intervallschachtelung (principle of) nested intervals
intuitiv intuitive
invariant (unveränderlich) invariant
invers (umgekehrt) inverse
inverse Matrix inverse matrix
inverse Rechenoperation inverse operation
inverser Wert inverse value
invertierbar invertible
irrational irrational
irrationale Zahl irrational number
Irrtum mistake, error
isolierter Punkt isolated point
Isomorphismus isomorphism
Istmaß actual size

J

Jahrgang age group
Jahrhundert century
jährlich yearly, annually
Jahrtausend millennium

Jahrzehnt decade
je per, each
Jota iota

K

Kalender calendar
Kalkül calculus
kalkulieren calculate, compute
Kalotte spherical cap
Kante edge
Kapazität capacity
Kapital principal
Kapitel chapter
Kardinalzahl cardinal number
kariert checkered
Karomuster checkerboard pattern
Karopapier graph paper
Karte chart
kartesisches Koordinatensystem Cartesian coordinate system
kartesisches Produkt Cartesian product
Kategorie category
Kathete side, leg
kaufmännisches Rechnen business arithmetic
Kegel cone
  abgeschnittener Kegel truncated cone
  gerader Kegel right cone
  schiefer Kegel oblique cone
  schräg abgeschnittener Kegel obliquely truncated cone
Kegelmantel lateral surface of a cone
Kegelschnitt conic section
Kegelstumpf frustum of a cone
  gerader Kreiskegelstumpf frustum of a right circular cone
Kehrwert inverse value, reciprocal value
Keil wedge
Keilwinkel dihedral angle
Kennzeichen characteristic, sign
Keplerbahn Kepler ellipse, elliptical path of planetary orbit
Kern core, kernel
Kette chain
Kettenbruch continued fraction
Kettenlinie catenary
Kettenregel chain rule
kippen tilt, tip
Kippwinkel angle of inclination

Klammer, eckige bracket (*Am.*), square bracket (*Brit.*)
Klammer, geschwungene brace
Klammer, runde parenthesis (*Am.*), bracket (*Brit.*)
Klasseneinteilung partition into classes
Klassenhäufigkeit cell frequency
Klassifizierung nach einem einzigen Merkmal one-way classification
klein small
kleiner oder gleich ($\leq$) less than or equal to
kleinster gemeinsamer Nenner least common denominator
kleinstes gemeinsames Vielfaches least common multiple
knapp tight, concise
Knoten knot, node
Knotenpunkt node of a curve
Koeffizient coefficient
Koeffizientenvergleich comparison of coefficients
kollineare Punkte collinear points
Kollinearität collinearity
Kolonne column
Kombination combination
Kombination mit (ohne) Wiederholung combination with (without) repetition
Kombinatorik combinatorial analysis
kombinieren combine
Komma decimal point, comma
kommensurabel commensurable
kommutativ commutative
kommutativer Körper commutative field
Kommutativgesetz commutative law
Kommutativität commutativity
Kompaß compass (navigator's instrument)
Kompaßpeilung compass bearing
komplanar coplanar
komplanare Geraden (in einer Ebene liegend) coplanar lines
Komplanarität coplanarity
Komplement (Ergänzung) complement
komplementäre Matrix complementary matrix
Komplementärwinkel complementary angle
komplexe Zahl complex number
Komponenten components
Komponentenzerlegung eines Vektors vector decomposition

Konfidenzbereich confidence region
Konfidenzintervall confidence interval
kongruent congruent
kongruent modulo m congruent modulo m
Kongruenz congruence
Kongruenzabbildung congruent mapping, congruent transformation
Kongruenzsätze für Dreiecke triangle congruence theorems
konjugiert komplexe Zahl conjugated complex number
konkav concave
Können (Fachkenntnis) skill
Konstante constant
konstantes Glied constant term
Konstruierbarkeit constructibility
Konstruktion construction
Konstruktion mit Zirkel und Lineal construction with ruler and compasses
kontinuierlich continuous
Kontinuum continuum
Kontinuumshypothese continuum hypothesis
kontradiktorisch (widerspruchsvoll) contradictory
Kontraposition contrapositive sentence
konträre Aussage inverse sentence
Kontrolle control, check
konvergent convergent
Konvergenz convergence
  gleichmäßige Konvergenz uniform convergence
Konvergenzkriterien convergence criteria
Konvergenzradius radius of convergence
konvergieren converge
konverse Implikation converse implication
konvex convex
konvexes Polygon (Vieleck) convex polygon
konzentrieren concentrate
konzentrisch concentric
konzyklisch concyclic
Koordinate coordinate
Koordinatenebene coordinate plane
Koordinatengeometrie coordinate geometry
Koordinatennullpunkt origin of coordinates
Koordinatensystem coordinate system
Koordinatenursprung origin of a coordinate plane

Kopf oder Zahl (*Österr.* **Kopf oder Adler**) heads or tails
Kopfrechnen mental calculation
Kopie copy
Korollar corollary
Körper field, body, solid, domain
Körper mit gleichem Rauminhalt solids of equal volume
Körpererweiterung field extension
Korrektur (Verbesserung) correction
Korrelation correlation
Korrespondenz correspondence
Kosekans cosecant
Kosinus cosine
Kosinusfunktion cosine function
Kosinussatz law of cosines
Kotangens cotangent
Kovariante covariant
Kovarianzanalyse covariance analysis
Kräfteparallelogramm parallelogram of forces
Kreis circle
  angeschriebener Kreis escribed circle
  eingeschriebener Kreis inscribed circle
  umgeschriebener Kreis circumscribed circle
Kreisausschnitt sector
Kreisbogen arc
Kreisdiagramm circle graph, circular chart
Kreisdurchmesser diameter
Kreisfläche area of a circle
Kreisflächeninhalt area of a circle
Kreisfunktion circular function (trigonometry)
Kreiskegel circular cone
Kreismittelpunkt center of circle
Kreispunkte concyclic points
Kreisradius radius of a circle
Kreisring annulus, circular ring
kreisrund circular
Kreisschar family of circles
Kreissegment segment of a circle
Kreissektor sector of a circle
Kreissehne chord
Kreisteilungsgleichung cyclotomic equation
Kreisumfang circumference of circle
Kreisviertel quadrant of a circle
Kreiszylinder circular cylinder
Kreuz cross
kreuzen intersect, cross

Kreuzprodukt cross product
Kreuzriß side view, profile
Kreuzung intersection, crossing
Kriterium criterion
krumm curved, bent, twisted
Krümmung (einer Kurve, einer Fläche) curvature
Krümmungsradius radius of curvature
kubieren cube, raise to the third power
Kubik cubic
kubisch cubic, cubical (curve, equation)
Kubus (Würfel) cube, regular hexahedron
Kubusverdopplung duplication of the cube
Kugel sphere
Kugelabschnitt spherical segment
Kugelabstand spherical distance
Kugelausschnitt spherical sector
Kugelgeometrie spherical geometry
kugelig spherical
Kugelkalotte spherical cap
Kugeloberfläche surface area of a sphere
künstlich herstellen synthesize
Kurs exchange rate, price, course, route (Strecke)
Kurve curve
  offene Kurve open curve
  geschlossene Kurve closed curve
Kurve dritten Grades curve of third degree, cubic curve
Kurve in Parameterdarstellung parametric curve
Kurvenintegral curve integral
Kurvenschar family of curves
kurz concise, short
kürzen cancel, reduce
kürzen von Brüchen reduce fractions to lower terms
kürzester Abstand shortest distance

L

Landesgrenze border
Landmessung land surveying
lang long
Länge length
Länge der Höhe length of an altitude
Länge des Kreisbogens arc length
Längeneinheit unit of length
Längenmaß linear measure

Langlebigkeit longevity
Laplacescher Entwicklungssatz Laplace expansion of a determinant
leer empty, null, void
Leere void, emptiness
leere Menge empty set, null set
Lehrsatz theorem
Leistung achievement, performance
Leistungsbeurteilung achievement evaluation
Leistungsfähigkeit efficiency
Leistungsnachweis certificate
leistungsorientiert achievement-oriented
Leitlinie directrix
lenken direct, steer
letzte Ziffer terminal digit, last digit
liegen to be situated, lie
Limes limit
Lineal ruler, straightedge
linear abhängig linearly dependant
linear unabhängig linearly independent
lineare Abbildung linear map(ping), linear transformation
lineare Algebra linear algebra
lineare Gleichung linear equation
lineare Regression linear regression
Linearkombination linear combination
Linie line
  ausgezogene Linie solid line
  punktierte Linie dotted line
  strichlierte Linie dashed line
Liniendiagramm line graph
linke Klammer left parenthesis *(Am.)*, left bracket *(Brit.)*
links left
Logarithmentafel logarithm table
logarithmische Gleichung logarithmic equation
logarithmische Kurve logarithmic curve
logarithmische Spirale logarithmic spiral
Logarithmus logarithm
  natürlicher Logarithmus natural logarithm
Logik logic
logischer Schluß logical deduction
löschen erase, delete
lösen solve
Lösung solution
Lot normal, perpendicular; plumb (Senkblei)
Lotebene perpendicular plane

lotrecht perpendicular
Lücke gap

M

Mächtigkeit cardinality, potency
magisch magic
magisches Quadrat magic square
mal (2 mal 3) times (2 times 3)
Malzeichen multiplication sign
Mangel dearth, shortage, deficiency
Mannigfaltigkeit manifold
Mantelfläche (Seitenfläche) lateral area (or surface)
Mantellinie (eines Kegels) slant height (of a cone)
Maß measure
Masse mass
Maßeinheit unit of measure
Maßstab scale, criterion
Matrix matrix
Matrixdarstellung matrix representation
Matrixschreibweise matrix notation
Matrixtransformation matrix transformation
Matrizenalgebra matrix algebra
Maximum (Hochpunkt) maximum point
Median (Zentralwert) median
mehrfach multiple, repeatedly
mehrmals repeatedly, several times
mehrmehrdeutige Abbildung many to many mapping
Mehrzahl plural
Meile mile
Menge set, collection
  abgeschlossene Menge closed set
  elementfremde Mengen disjoint sets
  geordnete Menge ordered set
  leere Menge null set
  ungeordnete Menge unordered set
Menge geordneter Paare set of ordered pairs
Mengenbegriff concept of a set
Mengenlehre (Mengentheorie) set theory
Merkmal (Charakterzug) trait
Meßfehler error of measurement
Methode der kleinsten Quadrate least squares method
Methode der unbestimmten Koeffizienten method of undetermined coefficients

metrischer Raum metric space
Milliarde (10^9) billion (*Am.*), milliard (*Brit.*)
Millimeterpapier graph paper
Million (10^6) million
mindest least
minimal (Mindest ...,) minimal
Minimum (Tiefpunkt) minimum point
Minuend minuend
Minuszeichen minus sign
Mißerfolg failure
Mitglied member
Mittagskreis (Meridian) meridian
Mitte middle
Mittel medium, median, mean, middle
Mitteldreieck triangle formed by the midpoints of sides of triangle
Mittelpunkt center (*Am.*), centre (*Brit.*), midpoint
Mittelpunkt des Inkreises incenter (*Am.*), incentre (*Brit.*)
Mittelpunkt des Umkreises circumcenter (*Am.*), circumcentre (*Brit.*)
Mittelung averaging
Mittelungsmethode averaging method
Mittelwert mean, average
  arithmetischer Mittelwert arithmetic mean
  geometrischer Mittelwert geometric mean
  gewichteter (gewogener) Mittelwert weighted mean
  harmonischer Mittelwert harmonic mean
Mittelwert der Stichprobe sample mean
Mittelwertsatz der Integralrechnung mean value theorem for integrals
mittlere Krümmung mean curvature
mittlere Proportionale mean proportional
mittlere quadratische Abweichung mean square deviation
Modell model, pattern
Modul module
Modus mode
monoton monotone
Monotoniegesetz monotonic law
Mosaikarbeit tessellation
Multiplikation multiplication
Multiplikationszeichen multiplication sign
multiplizieren (mit) multiply (by)
Muster pattern
Musterbeispiel sample

N

n-Eck n-gon
n-Flächner (Polyeder)   polyhedron of n faces
n-seitiges Eck   polyhedral angle
nacheinander   successively
Nachfolger   successor, descendant
nachprüfen   re-examine, check
nachrechnen   check a calculation
Nähe   nearness, proximity, neighborhood
nähern   approach
Näherung   approximation
Näherungskonstruktion   approximate construction
natürliche Reihenfolge   normal order
natürliche Zahl   natural number
natürlicher Logarithmus   natural logarithm
Nebenachse   minor axis
Nebenrechnung   auxiliary calculation
nebensächlich   minor, peripheral
Nebenwinkel   adjacent angle
Negation   negation
negativ   negative
negative Zahl   negative number
negatives Zeichen   negative sign, minus sign
Neigungswinkel   angle of inclination
Neilsche Parabel   Neil's parabola
Nenner   denominator
   kleinster gemeinsamer Nenner   least common denominator
Nettoeinkommen   net- earnings
Netz   net
neun (neunte)   nine (ninth)
Neuneck   nonagon
Neunerprobe   casting out nines
Neunpunktkreis (Feuerbachscher Kreis)   Nine Point Circle
Neuntel   ninth
neunzehn (neunzehnte)   nineteen (nineteenth)
neunzig (neunzigste)   ninety (ninetieth)
neutrales Element   neutral element
Newtonsches Näherungsverfahren   Newton's methods of approximation
Nicht-Euklidische Geometrie   non-Euclidean geometry
nichtentarteter Kegelschnitt   non-degenerate conic
nichtexistierend   nonexistent
nichtleer   nonempty, nonvoid
nichtlineare Korrelation   curvilinear correlation
nichtlösbar   insoluble, unsolvable
nichtparallel   nonparallel
nichtrational   irrational, nonrational
nichtsymmetrisch   asymmetric
nichttransitiv   nontransitive
niedrig   low
Niveau   level
Norm   norm
normale Geraden   perpendicular lines
Normalverteilung   normal distribution
normiertes Polynom   normalized polynomial
notwendig   necessary
notwendige Bedingung   necessary condition
n-seitiges Polyeder   polyhedron of n faces
Null   zero, naught
Null setzen   equate to zero
Nullage   zero position
Nullelement   zero element
Nullhypothese   null hypothesis
Nullmenge   void set, empty set, null set
Nullstelle eines Polynoms   zero of a polynomial
Nullstellenbestimmung bei Polynomen   calculation of zeros of polynomials
Nullstrahl   polar axis
Nullteiler   zero divisor
numerische Differentiation   numerical differentiation
numerische Integration   numerical integration
Nummer   number
nützen   be of use

O

oben   above, up, on top
ober   superior, upper
obere Grenze   upper limit
obere Schranke   upper bound
oberer Index   superscript
Oberfläche   surface
Oberflächeninhalt   surface area
oberhalb   above
Obersumme   upper sum
ohne gemeinsames Maß   incommensurable

Oktaeder (Achtflächner) octahedron
Oktalschreibweise octal notation
Optimierung optimization
Ordinalzahl ordinal number
Ordinate ordinate
Ordnung order
Ordnungszahl ordinal number
Orientierung orientation
Ort position, locus
orthogonal orthogonal
Ost east
Oszillation oscillation
oval (Oval) oval

P

Paar pair, couple
palindrome Zahl palindromic number
Parabel parabola
parabolische Fläche parabolic surface
parabolische Kurve parabolic curve
Paradoxon paradox
Parallele parallel
parallele Geraden parallel lines
Parallelität parallelism
Parallelogramm parallelogram
Parallelverschiebung parallel displacement, parallel translation
Parameter parameter
Parität parity
Partialbruch partial fraction
Partialbruchzerlegung partial fraction expansion
Partialsumme partial sum
partielle Ableitung partial derivative
partielle Differentiation partial differentiation
partielle Integration integration by parts
Pascalsches Dreieck Pascal's triangle
passen match
passend appropriate
Pauschalgebühr flat rate
Peanos Axiomensystem Peano's axiom system
Pentaeder pentahedron
Pentagonalzahl pentagonal number
perfekte Zahl perfect number
Periode period
periodisch periodic

periodische Dezimalzahl repeating decimal, recurring decimal
periodischer Dezimalbruch periodic decimal fraction
Permutation permutation
Perspektive perspective
Pfeil arrow
Pfeilspitze arrowhead
Pfund pound
Plan design, map, draft
Platzhalter place holder, variable
Pluszeichen plus sign, addition sign
Pol polar point
Polarachse polar axis
Polardreieck polar triangle
Polare polar line
Polarkoordinaten polar coordinates
Polarkreis polar circle
Polstelle pole
Polyeder (Vielflächner) polyhedron
Polyedereck polyhedral angle
Polygon (Vieleck) polygon
Polygonalzahl polygonal number
Polynom polynomial
Polynomialentwicklung multinomial expansion
Population population
positiv positive
positive Zahl positive number
positives Zeichen plus sign
Potenz power (as exponent)
Potenz eines Punktes bezüglich eines Kreises power of a point with respect to a circle
potenzieren raising to a power
Potenzmenge power set
Potenzpapier log-log paper
Potenzrechnung calculation with powers
Potenzreihe power series
prägnant concise, terse
Preisnachlaß discount
prim prime
Primfaktor prime factor
Primfaktorenzerlegung factorization into prime factors
primitive Einheitswurzel primitive root of unit
Primitivwurzel primitive root
Primzahl prime number
Primzahlenfolge sequence of prime numbers

Primzahlzwillinge prime pair, twin primes
Prinzip principle
Prisma prism
   dreiseitiges Prisma triangular prism
   gerades Prisma right prism
   rechteckiges Prisma rectangular prism
   schiefes Prisma oblique prism
Probe test, trial, check
probieren try, attempt
Problemlösen problem solving
Produkt product
Produkt von Vektoren vector product
   inneres Produkt inner (dot) product
   äußeres Produkt outer (cross) product
Produktregel product rule
Projektion projection
projektive Ebene projective plane
projektive Geometrie projective geometry
Projektivität projectivity
Proportion proportion
   direkt Proportion direct proportion
   indirekt Proportion indirect proportion
proportional proportional
protokollieren record
Prozent percent
Prozentrechnen percentage calculation
Prozentsatz percentage rate
Prozentwert (Prozentanteil) part
Prüfung examination
Ptolemäischer Lehrsatz Ptolemy's theorem
Punkt point, vertex
   Anfangspunkt initial point
   Endpunkt terminal point
Punktfolge sequence of points
punktiert dotted
Punktrichtungsgleichung der Geraden
     point-slope form of a line
Punktwolke scatter diagram
Pyramide pyramid
   abgeschnittene Pyramide truncated pyramid
   gerade Pyramide right pyramid
   quadratische Pyramide square based pyramid
   schiefe Pyramide oblique pyramid
   schräg abgeschnittene Pyramide obliquely truncated pyramid
Pyramidenstumpf (gerader) frustum of a pyramid (right)
Pythagoreischer Lehrsatz Pythagorean theorem
Pythagoreisches Zahlentripel Pythagorean triple

Q

Quader rectangular prism, cuboid
Quadrant (Viertelebene) quadrant
Quadrat square
   magisches Quadrat magic square
   vollständiges Quadrat perfect square
quadratisch quadratic
quadratische Gleichung quadratic equation
quadratischer Rest quadratic residue
Quadratkilometer square kilometer
Quadrattafel table of squares
Quadratur des Kreises squaring the circle
Quadratwurzel square root
Quadratwurzelziehen extract the square root of
Quadratzahl square number
quadrieren square
Quadrillion (10^{24}) septillion *(Am.)*, quadrillion *(Brit.)*
Quantifikator quantifier
Quantität quantity
Quartil (Streuungsmaß) quartile
Quelle source, origin
quer cross, transverse
Querschnitt cross cut, cross section
Querstrich horizontal line
Quersumme sum of the digits
quinäre Zahlendarstellung (mit der Basis 5) quinary notation
Quotient quotient
Quotientenkörper quotient field
Quotientenkriterium ratio test
Quotientenregel quotient rule

R

Rabatt discount
Radiant (*Zeichen*: rad) radian
Radikal radical
Radius (*pl.* Radien) radius (*pl.* radii)
Radius des Inkreises inradius
Radius des Inkreises (eines regelmäßigen Vielecks) apothem (of a polygon)
Radius des Umkreises circumradius, radius of circumscribed circle

Radix (Wurzel) root
radizieren extract a root
Radkurve cycloid
Rahmen frame
Rand frontier, boundary, border, edge, margin
Randverteilung marginal distribution
Randwertproblem boundary value problem
Rang rank
Rang einer Matrix rank of a matrix
rational machen rationalizing
rationale Zahl rational number
rationaler Bruch rational fraction
Raum space
Rauminhalt volume
Raummaß cubic measure
Raumwinkel tetrahedral angle
Raute rhombus
Realität reality
Realteil real part
Rechenaufgabe arithmetic problem
Rechenoperation arithmetical operation
Rechenschieber slide rule
Rechentabelle mathematical table
rechnen compute, calculate
Rechnung calculation, bill, check *(Am.)*
recht, rechts right
rechte Klammer right parenthesis *(Am.)*, right bracket *(Brit.)*
Rechteck rectangle
rechteckig rectangular
rechter Winkel right angle
Rechtseinselement right identity element
rechtsinvers right inverse
rechtsinverses Element right inverse element
rechtsseitige Distributivität right distributivity
rechtwinklig right-angled, orthogonal, perpendicular
rechtwinkliges Dreieck right triangle *(Am.)*, right-angled triangle *(Brit.)*
redundant (überflüssig) redundant, unnecessary
reelle Achse real axis
reelle Zahl real number
reelles Zahlensystem real number system
reflexiv reflexive
Regel rule

regelmäßiger Körper (platonischer Körper) regular solid (Platonic solid)
regelmäßiger Vielflächner (regulärer Polyeder) regular polyhedron
regelmäßiges Vieleck regular polygon
Regression regression
reguläres Polygon regular polygon
Reichweite coverage
reif ripe, mature
Reihe (Zeile) row
Reihe (Summe einer Folge) series
konvergente Reihe convergent series
divergente Reihe divergent series
Reihenfolge in order, in sequence
in dieser Reihenfolge respectively
in umgekehrter Reihenfolge in reverse order
rein pure, clean
rein imaginäre Zahl pure imaginary number
rein quadratische Gleichung pure quadratic equation
Rekursion recursion, recurrence
Rekursionsformel recursion formula
rekursive Funktion recursive function
Relation relation
relativ abgeschlossene Menge relatively closed set
relativ prime Zahlen relatively prime numbers
relativ widerspruchsfrei relatively consistent
relative Häufigkeit relative frequency
relative Wachstumsrate relative growth rate
relativer Fehler relative error
Residuensatz residue theorem
Rest rest, remainder, residual
Rest (bei Division) remainder
Restklasse residue class, coset
Restklassenkörper residue class field
Restklassenmodul residue class module
Restklassenring residue class ring
Resultat result, resultant
Resultierende (Vektorsumme) resultant (of vectors)
Reziproke reciprocal
reziproke Funktion reciprocal function
reziproker Wert reciprocal value
Rhombus rhombus
Richtung direction

Ringfläche torus
Riß projection, view
 Aufriß vertical projection
 Grundriß horizontal projection
 Schrägriß skew projection
Röhre tube, pipe
Röhrenfläche tubular surface
Rolle pulley
Rotationskörper solid of revolution
Rückentwicklung regression
Rückkehrpunkt cusp
rückläufig retrograde
Rücknahme withdrawal
Rücksicht with respect to, consideration
rückwärtszählen count backwards
runde Klammer parenthesis (*pl.* parentheses) (*Am.*), bracket (*Brit.*)
runden rounding off
Rundungsfehler rounding error

S

Sachkenntnis skill
sachlich objective
Sachrechnung practical problem
Sammlung collection
Satz theorem, sentence, proposition
Schachbrett checkerboard
Schachtelung nesting, nest
Schall sound
Schaltjahr leap year
Schar family, swarm, crowd
Schatten shadow
schätzen estimate, guess, appraise
Schätzung estimate, guess
schätzungsweise roughly, approximately
Schätzwert estimation
Scheffel bushel
scheinbar apparently
Scheinkorrelation illusory correlation
Scheitel (Scheitelpunkt) vertex, zenith
Scheitelwinkel vertical angles
Schema array, diagram, pattern
Schenkel side (of a right or isosceles triangle)
schieben move, push, slide
Schiebung translation
schief (schräg) skew, sloping, slanting
Schiefe skewness
schiefe Pyramide oblique pyramid

schiefer Kreiskegel oblique circular cone
schiefer Kreiszylinder oblique circular cylinder
Schleife loop
schließen close, include, enclose, involve
Schlinge loop
Schluß end, conclusion
Schlüsselzahl code number
Schlußfolgerung conclusion
schmal narrow
Schmiegebene osculating plane
Schnecke Limaçon
Schneckenlinie spiral, helix
schneidend intersecting, secant
schneidende Ebenen intersecting planes
schneidende Geraden intersecting lines
Schnelligkeit speed, rapidity, velocity
Schnitt cut, section, intersection
Schnittebene intersecting plane
Schnittpunkt point of intersection
Schnittwinkel zweier Ebenen bzw. Kanten dihedral angle
Schraffierung hatching lines, striations
Schräge slant, slope (Gefälle)
Schrägriß (Schrägansicht) skew projection
Schranke bound
 größte untere Schranke greatest lower bound
 kleinste obere Schranke least upper bound
Schreibweise notation
Schwäche weakness
Schwankung oscillation
Schwerlinie median (line)
Schwerpunkt centroid, center of gravity
Schwingungsweite amplitude
sechs (sechste) six (sixth)
Sechseck hexagon
Sechsflächner (Hexaeder) hexahedron
Sechstel sixth
sechzehn (sechzente) sixteen (sixteenth)
sechzig (sechzigste) sixty (sixtieth)
Segment segment of a circle
Sehne chord of a circle
Sehnenviereck inscribed quadrilateral
Seite side (of a polygon), face (of a solid)
Seitenansicht side view
Seitenfläche lateral surface, lateral face
Seitenhöhe slant height
Seitenhalbierende median of a triangle

Seitenkante lateral edge
Seitenlänge length of a side
Seitenpaar pair of sides
Sekans secant
Sekansfunktion secant function
Sekante secant (line)
Sektor sector
senkrecht perpendicular, normal, vertical
Senkungswinkel angle of depression
Sequenz sequence
Serie series
setzen put, place, set in position
Sexagesimalrechnung sexagesimal arithmetic
Sexagesimalsystem (Sechzigersystem) sexagesimal system of notation
sich gegenseitig ausschließende Ereignisse mutually exclusive events
sich häufen accumulate
sicheres Ereignis certain event
Sieb sieve
sieben (siebente) seven (seventh)
Siebeneck heptagon
Siebentel seventh
siebzehn (siebzehnte) seventeen (seventeenth)
Siebzehneck (17-Eck) seventeen sided polygon (17-gon)
siebzig (siebzigste) seventy (seventieth)
Signifikanzniveau level of significance
simultane Gleichungen simultaneous equations
singuläre Matrix singular matrix
singulärer Punkt singular point
Sinn sense
Sinnbild symbol
sinnlos absurd, meaningless
sinnvoll meaningful
Sinus sine
Sinusfunktion sine function
Sinussatz law of sines
Skalar (Zahl) scalar
Skalarprodukt scalar product, dot product
Skizze (Entwurf) sketch, rough draft, outline
skizzieren sketch
Spalt gap, split, slot
Spalte (Kolonne) column
Spannbreite span
Spanne span, interval
spannen stretch, span

Spannung tension
Spannweite range
Spat parallelepiped
Spatprodukt parallepidial product
Spektrum spectrum
Sphäre sphere
sphärisch spherical
sphärische Fläche spherical surface
sphärische Geometrie spherical geometry
sphärischer Winkel spherical angle
sphärisches Dreieck spherical triangle
Spiegel mirror
Spiegelbild reflected image
spiegeln reflect
Spiegelung (an einer Ebene) reflection (in a plane)
Spiegelungsachse axis of symmetry
Spiel game
Spielraum margin of error, amount of tolerance
Spirale, spiralförmig spiral
Spiralkurve spiral curve
spitz pointed, acute
Spitze vertex, point, summit, spire (Turm), apex
spitzer Winkel acute angle
spitzwinkliges Dreieck acute triangle
Sprung (Sprungstelle) jump
Spur (ein Körnchen) grain
Stabdiagramm bar graph
Staffelbild histogram
Standardabweichung standard deviation
ständig permanent, constant, continuous
Stärke strength
stärken strengthen
starr rigid, solid
Starrheit rigidity
Statistik statistics
statistischer Fehler statistical error
steigen ascend, increase
Steigerung increase
Steigungswinkel angle of elevation
steil steep
Stelle place
Stellen vertauschen juxtaposition
Stellenwert place value
Stereometrie solid geometry
Stern asterisk (*), star
Sternkurve asteroid
stetig continuous
stetige Progression continuous progression

stetige Verteilung continuous distribution
stetiger Prozeß continuous process
Stetigkeit continuity
Stetigkeitsaxiom continuity axiom
Stichprobe (random) sample
Stichprobenauswahl sample choose
Stichprobenerhebung sample survey, sampling
Stichprobenfehler sampling error
Stichprobenraum sample space
Stichprobenumfang sample size
stören disturb
Stoß impact, push
Strahl ray, half-line
Strahlenbüschel pencil of lines
Strahlensatz theorem of proportional segments
streben (nach) strive (for), converge
Strecke line segment
Streckensymmetrale perpendicular bisector of line segment
Streckenzug broken line
Streckung stretch, enlargement
streng exact, rigorous, precise
strenger Beweis rigorous proof
Streubild scatter diagram
Streuung dispersion, scattering, variation
Strich (') prime (mark)
  a', a'' a prime, a double prime
strichliert dashed
Strichliste tally chart
Stufe step
Stufenfunktion step function
stufenweise step by step
Stumpf frustum
  Kegelstumpf frustum of a cone
stumpf obtuse, dull
stumpfer Winkel obtuse angle
stumpfwinkliges Dreieck obtuse triangle
Stundenzeiger hour hand
stürzen transpose (a matrix)
Substitution substitution
Substitutionsregel substitution formula
Subtrahend subtrahend
subtrahieren subtract
Subtraktion subtraction
Subtraktionszeichen subtraction sign
suchen search, seek, require, look for
Süden south
Südpol south pole
sukzessiv (aufeinanderfolgend) successive

Summand addend
Summe sum
Summenzeichen (Σ) summation sign
summieren add
supplementär supplementary
Supplementärwinkel supplementary angle
surjektive Abbildung onto function
Symbolik symbolism
symbolische Darstellung symbolic representation
Symmetrale line of symmetry, bisector
Symmetrie symmetry
Symmetrieachse axis of symmetry
Symmetrieebene plane of symmetry
Symmetriegerade line symmetry
symmetrisch symmetrical
symmetrische Gleichung symmetric equation
Synthese synthesis
System (von Gleichungen) system (of equations)
systematisch systematic

T

t-**Verteilung** *t*-distribution
tabellarisch tabular
Tabellarisierung tabulation
Tabelle chart, table
Tafel table, chalkboard, projection plane
Tangens tangent
Tangensfunktion tangent function
Tangente tangent (line)
Tangentensatz law of tangents
Tangentensechseck circumscribed hexagon
Tangentensehnenwinkel tan-chord angle (angle formed by a tangent and a chord)
Tangentenvektor tangent vector
Tangentenvieleck circumscribed polygon
tangential tangent, tangential
Tangentialebene tangent plane
Tarif price, rate
Tasterzirkel (Greifzirkel) calipers
Tauglichkeit suitability, fitness
tausend (tausendste) thousand (thousandth)
Tausendstel thousandth
Tautologie tautology

Taylor-Reihe Taylor series
Teil part, portion
Teilableitung partial differentiation
Teilbarkeit divisibility
Teilbarkeitskriterium criterion for divisibility
Teilbarkeitsregeln rules for divisibility
Teilbruch partial fraction
teilen share, divide
  in drei gleiche Teile teilen trisect, divide into three equal parts
Teiler divisor
  größter gemeinsamer Teiler greatest common divisor
teilerfremd relatively prime
Teilfolge subsequence
Teilmenge subset
Teilung division
Teilungszahl quotient
teilweise partial, by parts
Teleskop telescope
teleskopisch telescopic
Tempo rate of speed
Tendenz tendency
Term term
  gleichnamiger Term like term
Testergebnis test score
Tetraeder (Vierflächner) tetrahedron
tetraedisch tetrahedral
Thema topic
theoretisch theoretical
Theorie theory
thermisch thermal
These thesis
tief deep
Tiefe depth
tiefgestellte Zahl subscript
Tiefpunkt minimum point
Ton sound, tone
Topologie topology
Torus torus
Totalbetrag total amount
Totalkörper total field, entire field
träg inert
Trägheitsgesetz law of inertia
transitiv transitive
Transitivität transitivity
Transitivitätsgesetz law of transitivity
transponieren transpose
transzendente Zahl transcendental number
Trapez trapezoid *(Am.)*, trapezium *(Brit.)*

treffen meet
treiben drive, push, force, set in motion, propel, work, operate
Trennbarkeit separability
trennen separate
Triangularzahl triangular number
triangulieren triangulate
Trigonometrie trigonometry
  ebene Trigonometrie plane trigonometry
  sphärische Trigonometrie spherical trigonometry
trigonometrische Funktionen trigonometric functions
Trillion (10^{18}) quintillion *(Am.)*, trillion *(Brit.)*
Trinom trinomial
Tripel triple
Trisektion trisection
trivial trivial
Trugschluß fallacy
Typ type
typisch typical
Typus type

U

über over, above
überabzählbar uncountable
überall dicht everywhere dense
überall stetig completely continuous
überbleibender Rest remainder
Überblick overview, survey
überblicken survey
Überdeckung cover, covering
überflüssig superfluous, unnecessary, excess, surplus, redundant
übergreifen overlap
überlagern overlay, overlap
Überlagerung covering, overlapping, superposition
überlappend (Dreiecke) overlapping (triangles)
überlegen consider, think about
übermäßig excessive
überprüfen review, check, examine
Überprüfung review, examination, check
übersteigen exceed
überstumpf (erhaben) reflex
Übertragung transfer
überzählig superfluous

übrig remaining
übrigbleiben remain
Übung drill
Übungsaufgabe exercise
Ufer bank (of river), boundary
uferlos boundless
Uhrzeiger hand of a clock or watch
Uhrzeigersinn clockwise direction
Umdrehung revolution, turn
Umdrehungsachse axis of revolution
Umdrehungspunkt center of revolution
Umdrehungszahl number of revolutions
Umfang perimeter, circumference
umfassend all inclusive, comprehensive
Umformung transformation, conversion
Umfrage poll
Umgebung environment, neighborhood
umgekehrte Implikation converse implication
umgekehrte Reihenfolge reverse order
umgekehrtes Verhältnis reciprocal ratio
umgruppieren regroup, rearrange
umhüllen envelope
umkehrbar reversible
umkehrbar eindeutige Beziehung one-to-one correspondence
umkehren invert, reverse
Umkehrformel inversion formula
Umkehrsatz inverse theorem
Umkehrung converse, reversal, inversion
Umkreis circumscribed circle, circumcircle
umkreisen encircle
Umkreismittelpunkt circumcenter *(Am.)*, circumcentre *(Brit.)*
Umkreisradius circumradius
umlaufen revolve, circulate
Umlaufgeschwindigkeit velocity of revolution
Umlaufszahl number of revolutions
Umlaufzeit period of revolution
Umnumerierung renumbering
Umordnung rearrangement
Umrandung bordering
umrechnen convert
Umrechnung (Konvertierung) conversion
Umrechnungstabelle conversion table
Umriß (Überblick) outline
umschreiben circumscribe, rewrite
umwandeln convert, change, transform
Umwandlung conversion, change, transformation

Umwandlung von Maßeinheiten conversion of units
unabhängig independent
unabhängige Ereignisse independent events
unabhängige Variable independent variable
unbeabsichtigt accidental
unbedingt unconditional, absolutely
unbegrenzt unlimited, unbounded, limitless, boundless
unbekannt unknown
unberechenbar incalculable, unpredictable
unbeschränkt unbounded, indefinitely, limitless
unbeschränkte Menge unbounded set
unbeschränktes Intervall unbounded interval
unbestimmte Gleichung indeterminate equation
unbestimmte Zahl arbitrary number
unbestimmter Ausdruck indeterminate form
unbestimmter Koeffizient undertermined coefficient
unbestimmtes Gleichungssystem indeterminate system of equations
unbestimmtes Integral indefinite integral
Unbestimmtheit uncertainty
unbeweisbar unprovable
unbewiesen unproved
unbiegsam inflexible, rigid
undefinierbar indefinable
undefiniert undefined
unechter Bruch improper fraction
uneigentlicher Bruch improper fraction
uneigentliches Integral improper integral
unendlich infinite
Unendlichkeit infinity
ungefähr approximate
ungekürzt unabridged
ungenügend insufficient, unsatisfactory
ungeordnete Menge unordered set
ungerade (Zahl) odd (number)
ungerichtet undirected
ungeteilt undivided
Ungewißheit uncertainty
ungleich unequal
Ungleichheit inequality
ungleichseitig (Dreieck) scalene (triangle)

ungültig invalid
ungünstig unfavorable
unitär (einheitlich) unitary
unkürzbar irreducible
unlösbar unsolvable, insoluble
unlösbare Gleichung unsolvable equation
unlösbares (unverträgliches) Gleichungssystem inconsistent equations
Unordnung disorder
unsicher uncertain
unsinnig absurd
unstetig discontinuous
Unstetigkeitsstelle point of discontinuity
unsymmetrisch asymmetric, skew
unten below
unter under, lower, inferior
untere Grenze lower limit
untere Schranke lower bound
Untergruppe subgroup
Unterhaltung entertainment, recreation
Untermenge subset
   echte Untermenge proper subset
   unechte Untermenge improper subset
Unterraum subspace
Unterschied difference
unterstützen foster, support
untersuchen inspect, check, investigate
unvereinbar inconsistent
Unvereinbarkeit inconsistency
unverfälscht unbiased
unverträglich incompatible
unvorhersehbar unpredictable
unwahrscheinlich improbable
unzählbar innumerable, uncountable
unzugänglich inaccessible
Urbild inverse image
Ursprung origin

V

variabel (veränderlich) variable
Variable variable
Varianzanalyse analysis of variance
Vektor vector
Vektoraddition vector addition
Vektoralgebra vector algebra
Vektorprodukt vector product
Vektorraum vector space
Vektorrechnung vector calculations
Vektorsumme vector sum

verallgemeinern generalize
veränderlich (Veränderliche) variable
Veranschaulichung graphic representation, visualization
verbessern improve, correct
Verbesserung improvement, correction
verbinden join, connect
Verbindungsgesetz associative law
Verbindungspunkt connecting point
Verdichtung compression, condensation
Verdopplung duplication
Veredelung refinement
vereinfachen simplify
Vereinfachung simplification
vereinigen unite, join, combine
Vereinigung union
Vereinigungsmenge set union, union of sets
verengen constrict, narrow
Verfahren procedure
Verfeinerung refinement
verfügbar available
vergleichen compare, match
Vergleichskriterium comparison test
vergrößern increase, enlarge, magnify
Verhältnis ratio, proportion
Verhältnisgleichung proportion
verhindern prevent
verkehrt reverse, inverse, inverted
verkleinern reduce, make smaller
Verkürzungsverhältnis reduction factor
Verlängerung prolongation
Verlangsamung retardation
Verlust loss
vermehren increase
Vermehrung increase
vermeiden (ausweichen) avoid
Vermessung (Land) surveying
vermindern decrease, reduce, diminish
vermuten guess, imagine, expect (erwarten)
Vermutung conjecture, guess, expectation
vernachlässigen neglect
Verneinungsgesetz law of negation
verpflanzen transplant, transfer
verrechnen miscalculate
verrücken displace
verschieben displace, move, shift
verschieden distinct
Verschlüsselung coding
versetzen shift, transpose, transfer

Versetzung shifting, transposition, permutation
Versicherungsmathematik actuarial theory
Versicherungsmathematiker actuary
Versicherungsstatistik insurance statistics
versorgen supply
verstärken reinforce, strengthen
Versuch trial, experiment, attempt, test
versuchen attempt, try
vertauschen exchange, interchange, transpose, commute, permute
Vertauschungsgesetz commutative law
Verteilung distribution, spread, sharing
Verteilungsgesetz distributive law
vertikal vertical
Vertikalebene vertical plane
verträglich (kompatibel) compatible, consistent
vervielfachen multiply
vervollständigen complete
verwenden apply
verwerfen reject
verwirklichen realize
Verwirklichung realization
verzerrte (verfälschte) Stichprobe biased sample
Verzerrung distortion
Verzinsung yield of interest
Verzweigung ramification
vibrieren vibrate
viel many
Vieleck (Polygon) polygon
Vieleckszahl polygonal number
Vielfaches multiple
  kleinstes gemeinsames Vielfaches least common multiple
Vielflächner (Polyeder) polyhedron
vier (vierte) four (fourth)
Viereck quadrangle, quadrilateral
vierfach fourfold, quadruple
Viertel quarter, fourth
vierzehn (vierzehnte) fourteen (fourteenth)
vierzig (vierzigste) forty (fortieth)
Vietascher Wurzelsatz Vieta's formulae
vollkommen perfect
vollkommene Zahl perfect number
Vollkreis complete circle
vollständige dritte Potenz perfect cube

vollständige Induktion mathematical induction
vollständiges Quadrat perfect square
Vollständigkeit completeness
Volumen volume
Volumseinheit cubic unit
vorausgesetzt (daß) provided (that), on condition that
voraussetzen (annehmen) assume, provide
Vorbereitung preparatory
Vorderansicht front view
Vorderglied antecedent
Vordergrund foreground
Vorgänger antecedent, predecessor
vorgehen proceed
vorher (früher) previously
vorherig previously
Vorlage (Muster) pattern
vorrücken advance, move forward
Vorschlag proposition, suggestion
vorschlagen propose
Vorschrift instructions, rule, regulation
vorstellen present, represent, visualize
Vorzahl coefficient
Vorzeichen sign
Vorzeichenänderung change of sign

W

waagrecht horizontal, level
wachsen grow, increase
wachsende Folge ascending sequence
wachsende Funktion increasing function
Wachstum growth
Wachstumsgeschwindigkeit rate of growth
Wahl choice, selection, vote
wahllos random
wahr true, correct
Wahrheitstafel truth table
Wahrheitswert truth value
Wahrscheinlichkeit probability
Wahrscheinlichkeitsrechnung theory of probability, calculus of probability
Wahrscheinlichkeitsverteilung probability distribution
Wechselbeziehung correlation
wechselseitig mutual
Weg way, path, route

Weite width, breadth, distance
Welle wave
wenden turn
Wendepunkt point of inflection
Werkzeug tool
Wert value, worth
Wertebereich range of values
Wertebereich einer Funktion range of a function
Wertung score
Widerrufung withdrawal
widersinnig absurd
Widerspruch contradiction
  Gesetz vom Widerspruch law of contradiction
  im Widerspruch stehen zu be inconsistent with
Widerspruchsbeweis indirect proof
Widerspruchsfreiheit consistency
Wiederholung repetition
Wiederkehr recurrence
wiegen weigh
windschiefe Geraden skew lines
Winkel angle
  anliegender Winkel adjacent angle
  Außenwinkel exterior angle
  erhabener Winkel reflex angle
  eingeschlossener Winkel included angle
  gegenüberliegender Winkel opposite angle
  gestreckter Winkel straight angle
  rechter Winkel right angle
  spitzer Winkel acute angle
  stumpfer Winkel obtuse angle
Winkel-Dreiteilung trisection of an angle
Winkelhalbierende angle bisector, bisector of an angle
Winkelgrad degree of an angle
Winkelmesser protractor
Winkelsymmetrale angle bisector, bisector of an angle
Wirksamkeit (Effizienz) efficiency
Wissen knowledge
wissenschaftliche Untersuchung research
wohldefiniert well-defined
wohlgeordnete Menge well ordered set
wünschenswert desirable
Wurfbahn trajectory
Würfel cube
Würfelverdopplung duplication of a cube
Wurzel (Quadratwurzel) root, radical (square root)

Wurzelgleichung radical equation
Wurzelkriterium root test
Wurzelrechnung calculation with roots
Wurzelspirale radical spiral
Wurzelzahl radical number
Wurzelzeichen radical sign

X

x-Achse x-axis
xy-Ebene xy-plane

Y

y-Achse y-axis

Z

Zahl number
  ganze Zahl whole number, integer
  gemischte Zahl mixed number
  gerade Zahl even number
  imaginäre Zahl imaginary number
  irrationale Zahl irrational number
  komplexe Zahl complex number
  natürliche Zahl natural number
  negative Zahl negative number
  positive Zahl positive number
  rationale Zahl rational number
  reelle Zahl real number
  transzendente Zahl transcendental number
  ungerade Zahl odd number
  vierstellige Zahl four-digit number
  zusammengesetzte Zahl composite number
zählen count
  rückwärts zählen count backwards
Zahlenfolge sequence of numbers
Zahlengerade number line
Zahlenmenge set of numbers
Zahlenreihe series of numbers
Zahlenstrahl number ray
Zahlentheorie number theory, theory of numbers
Zahlentripel (teilerfremdes) number triple (primitive)
Zahlenwert numerical value

Zähler numerator
zehn (zehnte) ten (tenth)
Zehneck (Dekagon) decagon
Zehnerbasis base ten
Zehnerbruch decimal fraction
Zehnergruppe decade
Zehnerpotenz power of ten
Zehnerstelle ten's place
Zehnersystem decimal system
Zehnerzahl decimal number
Zehnflächner decahedron
Zehntel tenth
Zeichen der Durchschnittsbildung ($\cap$) sign of intersection
Zeichen der Elementbeziehung ($\in$) sign of membership relation
Zeichen der Vereinigung ($\cup$) sign of union
zeichnen draw, sketch, design, plot
zeigen show, demonstrate
Zeile row
Zeitplan schedule
Zeitrechnung chronology
Zenit zenith
zentral central
Zentralwert median
Zentralwinkel central angle
Zentrum center (*Am.*), centre (*Brit.*)
zerlegbar (in Faktoren) factorable
zerlegen decompose, factor
Zerlegung decomposition, dissection, factoring
ziehen draw, extract (a root)
Ziehen mit (ohne) Zurücklegen drawing with (without) replacement
Ziel aim, goal, target
Zielbereich range
Ziffer figure, digit
Ziffernsumme (Quersumme) sum of the digits
Zinsen interest
  einfache Zinsen simple interest
  4 % Zinsen 4 % interest
Zinseszinsen compound interest
Zinsperiode interest period
Zinsrate (Zinssatz) rate of interest
Zirkel pair of compasses
zufällig random
zufällige Reihenfolge random order
zufälliger Fehler random error
zufälliges Ereignis random event
Zufallsauswahl random sample
Zufallsvariable random variable
Zufallszahl random number
zufrieden content, satisfied
Zug path, circuit, track, pull, tension
zugehörig belonging, accompanying
Zunahme increase, growth
zunehmen increase, grow
Zuordnung correlation, correspondent
zurücklegen replace
zurückziehen withdraw
„zusammenfallender Zirkel" pair of collapsible compasses
Zusammenfassung summary
zusammengesetzte Zahl composite number
zusammenhängend connected
zustandebringen (leisten) achieve
zuteilen (Aufgabe) assign (to), give (to)
Zuverlässigkeit reliability
Zuweisung assignment
zwanzig (zwanzigste) twenty (twentieth)
Zwanzigflächner (Ikosaeder) icosahedron
Zweck purpose
zwei (zweite) two (second)
zweideutig (unklar) ambiguous
zweidimensional two-dimensional
Zweiersystem binary system
zweifach double
Zweig branch
zweimal twice
zweiseitig bilateral
zweistellige (zweiziffrige) ganze Zahl two-digit integer
zweitens secondly
zwischen between
Zwischenwertsatz intermediate value theorem
zwölf (zwölfte) twelve (twelfth)
Zwölfeck (Dodekagon) dodecagon
Zwölfflächner (Dodekaeder) dodecahedron
Zwölftel twelfth
zyklisch cyclic
zyklische Gruppe cyclic group
zyklische Permutation cyclic permutation
Zykloide cycloid
Zyklus cycle

Zylinder cylinder
  abgeschnittener Zylinder truncated cylinder
  gerader Zylinder right cylinder
  Kreiszylinder circular cylinder
  schiefer Zylinder oblique cylinder
  schräg abgeschnittener Zylinder obliquely truncated cylinder

Zylinderoberfläche cylindrical surface

3. Teil
Schreib- und Sprechweise mathematischer Ausdrücke

Numbers and Sets of Numbers

Zahlen und Zahlenmengen

Numbers

In both languages all digits are written the same manner exept for 1 and 7.

1, 7   1, 7

Zahlen

In beiden Sprachen werden alle Ziffern gleich geschrieben, ausgenommen 1 und 7.

U. S. Decimal System

one	10^0
ten	10^1
one hundred	10^2
one thousand	10^3
one million	10^6
one **billion**	10^9
one trillion	10^{12}
one quadrillion	10^{15}
one quintillion	10^{18}
one sextillion	10^{21}
one septillion	10^{24}
one octillion	10^{27}
one nonillion	10^{30}

Note: There are **no milliards** in the U. S. Decimal System!

Read the number:
35 billion 875 million
12 thousand five

35,875,012,005 *(Am.)*
35 875 012 005

Commas for periods of three digits are used to help read a number.

Das Dezimalsystem (Europa)

eins
zehn
einhundert
eintausend
eine Million
eine **Milliarde**
eine Billion
eine Billiarde
eine Trillion
eine Trilliarde
eine Quadrillion
eine Quadrilliarde
eine Quintillion

Lies die Zahl:
35 Milliarden 875 Millionen
12 tausend fünf

Mit Hilfe von Zwischenräumen werden die Ziffern in Dreiergruppen gegliedert.

Sets of numbers

set of whole numbers	$\mathbb{W} = \{0,1,2,3,\ldots\} = \mathbb{N}$
set of natural numbers	$\mathbb{N} = \{1,2,3,\ldots\} = \mathbb{N}^*$
set of integers	$\mathbb{Z} = \{\ldots,-1,0,+1,\ldots\}$
set of rational numbers	$\mathbb{Q}$
set of irrational numbers	$\mathbb{I}$
set of real numbers	$\mathbb{R} = \mathbb{Q} \cup \mathbb{I}$
set of imaginary numbers	$\mathbb{I}m$
set of complex numbers	$\mathbb{C}$

Zahlenmengen

Menge der natürlichen Zahlen
Menge der natürlichen Zahlen ohne Null
Menge der ganzen Zahlen
Menge der rationalen Zahlen
Menge der irrationalen Zahlen
Menge der reellen Zahlen
Menge der imaginären Zahlen
Menge der komplexen Zahlen

Special sets of numbers		**Besondere Zahlenmengen**
set of non-negative even integers	$\{0,2,4,6,8,\ldots\}$	Menge der geraden natürlichen Zahlen
set of positive odd integers	$\{1,3,5,7,9,\ldots\}$	Menge der ungeraden natürlichen Zahlen
set of positive multiples of 4	$\{4,8,12,16,\ldots\}$	Menge der positiven Vielfachen von 4
set of positive divisors of 10	$\{1,2,5,10\}$	Menge der positiven Teiler von 10
Representation of the (real) numbers on a **number line**.	$\xleftarrow{\;-2\;-1\;\;0\;+1\;+2\;}$	Darstellung der (reellen) Zahlen auf der **Zahlengeraden**.

Calculation Terms

Fachausdrücke der Rechenoperationen

Addition

a plus b equals c $\qquad a + b = c$
\ / |
addends   sum

Addition

a plus b ist gleich c
\ / |
Summanden   Summe

Subtraction

a minus b equals c $\qquad a - b = c$
| \ \
minuend subtrahend difference

Subtraktion

a minus b ist gleich c
| \ \
Minuend Subtrahend Differenz

Multiplication

a times b equals c $\qquad a \times b = c \qquad a \cdot b = c$
\ / |
factors   product

Multiplikation

a mal b ist gleich c
\ / |
Faktoren   Produkt

Division

a divided by b equals c $\qquad a \div b = c \qquad a : b = c$
| | |
dividend divisor quotient

Division

a dividiert durch b ist gleich c
| | |
Dividend   Divisor   Quotient

Raising to a power

a to the nth power $\qquad\qquad a^n$
a to the nth
the nth power of a
 $\quad a^n\ldots$ power
 $\quad a\ldots$ base
 $\quad n\ldots$ exponent

Potenzieren

a hoch n
a zur n-ten
n-te Potenz von a
 $\quad a^n\ldots$ Potenz
 $\quad a\ldots$ Basis (Grundzahl)
 $\quad n\ldots$ Exponent (Hochzahl)

Extracting the root

the nth root of a $\qquad\qquad \sqrt[n]{a}$
 $\quad a\ldots$ radicand
 $\quad n\ldots$ index

Radizieren (Wurzelziehen)

n-te Wurzel aus a
 $\quad a\ldots$ Radikand
 $\quad n\ldots$ Wurzelexponent

Schreib- und Sprechweise mathematischer Ausdrücke

Spelling of Numbers

Decimals

. decimal point		
point seven (seven tenths)	.7	
four hundred fifty-seven point six	457.6	
repeating (periodic) decimals		
point three five repeating	$\overline{.35} = .353535\ldots$	

$$.7\overline{3}$$
$$/ \quad \backslash$$
non-repeating   repeating

Fractions

a over b	$\dfrac{a}{b} \quad (b \neq 0)$
a divided by b	
three fourths	$\dfrac{3}{4}$
3 ... numerator	
4 ... denominator	
proper fraction	$\dfrac{2}{3} < 1$
improper fraction	$\dfrac{7}{6} > 1$
mixed number	$2\dfrac{3}{4}$
decimal fraction (denominator is a power of 10)	$\dfrac{7}{10}$
unit fraction (numerator is 1)	$\dfrac{1}{8}$
complex fraction	$\dfrac{\tfrac{2}{3}}{\tfrac{4}{5}}$
continued fraction	$1 + \cfrac{1}{1 + \cfrac{1}{2 + \cfrac{1}{3\ldots}}}$

Positive and negative numbers

positive three (plus three)	$(+3)$
negative five (minus five)	(-5)
two minus negative five	$2 - (-5)$
the absolute value of x	$\lvert x \rvert$
or: absolute x	

Sprechweise von Zahlenausdrücken

Dezimalzahlen

, Komma	
Null Komma sieben (sieben Zehntel)	0,7
vierhundertsiebenundfünfzig Komma sechs	457,6
periodische Dezimalzahlen	
Null Komma fünfunddreißig periodisch	$0,\overset{..}{3}\overset{..}{5} = 0,353535\ldots$

$$0,7\overset{\bullet}{3}$$
$$/ \quad \backslash$$
Vorperiode   Periode

Brüche

a durch b	
a dividiert durch b	
drei Viertel	
3 ... Zähler	
4 ... Nenner	
echter Bruch	
unechter Bruch	
gemischte Zahl	
Dezimalbruch (Nenner ist eine Zehnerpotenz)	
Stammbruch (Zähler ist 1)	
Doppelbruch	
Kettenbruch	

Positive und negative Zahlen

plus drei	
minus fünf	
zwei minus minus fünf	
der absolute Betrag von x	
oder: der Betrag von x	

Powers, root numbers, irrationals | | ## Potenzen, Wurzeln, irrationale Zahlen

five squared or: five to the second power	5^2	fünf zum Quadrat oder: fünf hoch zwei
two to the minus seventh power	2^{-7}	zwei hoch minus sieben
perfect square	25	Quadratzahl
square root of two	$\sqrt{2}$	(Quadrat)Wurzel aus zwei
cube root of four	$\sqrt[3]{4}$	dritte Wurzel aus vier
the fourth root of five	$\sqrt[4]{5}$	vierte Wurzel aus fünf
e = 2.71 ... is the Euler number (base of the natural logarithm)	e	e = 2,71 ... ist die Eulersche Zahl (Basis des natürlichen Logarithmus)
π = 3.14... (read π as "pie") Ratio of the circumference of a circle to its diameter.	π	π = 3,14... Verhältnis des Kreisumfangs zum Durchmesser.

Complex numbers | | ## Komplexe Zahlen

complex plane defined by the real axis (unit 1) and the imaginary axis (unit i)	(diagram: Im/R axes with units i and 1)	Gaußsche Zahlenebene festgelegt durch die reelle Achse (Einheit 1) und die imaginäre Achse (Einheit i)
i squared equals –1	$i^2 = -1$	i zum Quadrat ist gleich –1
imaginary number "five i"	$5i$	imaginäre Zahl „fünf i"
complex number a ... real part b ... imaginary part (cartesian coordinates)	$z = a + bi$	komplexe Zahl a ... Realteil b ... Imaginärteil (kartesische Koordinaten)
z and z^* are a conjugate pair of complex numbers	$z = a + bi$ $z^* = a - bi$	z und z^* sind ein konjugiert komplexes Zahlenpaar
polar coordinates r ... the absolute value of z φ ... the argument of z	$z = (r, \varphi)$	Polarkoordinatendarstellung r ... der Betrag von z φ ... das Argument von z

Divisors and Multiples | | ## Teiler und Vielfache

b divides a b does not divide a	$b \mid a$ $b \nmid a$	b ist ein Teiler von a b ist kein Teiler von a
greatest common divisor (g.c.d).	g.c.d. (12, 18) = 6 ggT (12, 18) = 6	größter gemeinsamer Teiler (ggT)
g.c.d. $(a, b) = 1 \rightarrow a$ und b are relatively prime		ggT $(a, b) = 1 \rightarrow a$ und b sind teilerfremd oder relativ prim
least common multiple (l.c.m.)	l.c.m. (6, 8) = 24 kgV (6, 8) = 24	kleinstes gemeinsames Vielfaches (kgV)

Reading Mathematical Expressions		Sprechweise von Rechenausdrücken
Two plus three equals five. The sum of two and three is five.	$2 + 3 = 5$	Zwei plus drei ist fünf. Die Summe von zwei und drei ist fünf.
Twelve minus seven equals five. The difference between twelve and seven is five.	$12 - 7 = 5$	Zwölf minus sieben ist fünf. Die Differenz von zwölf und sieben ist fünf.
Negative four minus positive two equals negative six.	$(-4) - (+2) = -6$	Minus vier minus plus zwei ist gleich minus sechs.
Two multiplied by eight is sixteen. Two times eight equals sixteen. The product of two and eight is sixteen.	$2 \times 8 = 16 \quad 2 \cdot 8 = 16$	Zwei mal acht ist sechzehn. Das Produkt von zwei und acht ist sechzehn.
Eight divided by two is four. The quotient of eight divided by two is four.	$8 \div 2 = 4 \quad 8 : 2 = 4$	Acht dividiert durch zwei ist vier. Der Quotient von acht und zwei ist vier.
$17 \div 3 = 5$ remainder 2 Seventeen divided by three is five with a remainder of two.		$17 : 3 = 5$ 2 R Siebzehn dividiert durch drei ist fünf, Rest zwei.
Two to the third power is eight. Two cubed equals eight.	$2^3 = 8$	Zwei zur dritten (Potenz) ist acht. Zwei hoch drei ist acht.
a to the third (power) times b squared times c to the fifth (power) or: a cubed, b squared, c to the fifth	$a^3 \cdot b^2 \cdot c^5$	a hoch drei mal b hoch zwei mal c hoch fünf
Two x minus five equals nine. Two x minus five is greater than or equal to nine.	$2x - 5 = 9$ $2x - 5 \geq 9$	Zwei x minus fünf ist neun. Zwei x minus fünf ist größer oder gleich neun.
x to the minus three equals one over x to the third (power).	$x^{-3} = \dfrac{1}{x^3}$	x hoch minus drei ist gleich eins dividiert durch x hoch drei.
a to the two-thirds equals the cube root of a squared.	$a^{\frac{2}{3}} = \sqrt[3]{a^2}$	a hoch zwei Drittel ist gleich der dritten Wurzel aus a zum Quadrat.
three times the square root of two, over five	$\dfrac{3\sqrt{2}}{5}$	drei mal Quadratwurzel aus zwei dividiert durch fünf
x cubed over (or: divided by) the fourth root of five	$\dfrac{x^3}{\sqrt[4]{5}}$	x hoch drei dividiert durch die vierte Wurzel aus fünf

Different kinds of brackets | ## Verschiedene Arten von Klammern

( ) and [ ] are symbols of grouping used to tell which operation is to be performed first considering that the usual arithmetic order is not maintained: Multiplication/Division before Addition/Subtraction.

( ) und [ ] sind Symbole, die anzeigen, welche Rechenoperation zuerst durchgeführt werden muß, wenn die übliche Reihenfolge Multiplikation/Division vor Addition/Subtraktion nicht eingehalten wird.

parentheses *(Am.)*, brackets *(Brit.)*	( )	runde Klammern
brackets *(Am.)*, square brackets *(Brit.)*	[ ]	eckige Klammern
braces	{ }	geschwungene Klammern
two bracket *a* minus parenthesis three plus *b* close parenthesis close bracket *(Am.)* or: two square bracket *a* minus bracket three plus *b* close bracket close square bracket *(Brit.)*	$2[a-(3+b)]$	zwei mal eckige Klammer auf, *a* minus runde Klammer auf, drei plus *b*, runde und eckige Klammer geschlossen
the quantitiy *a* plus *b* to the fourth power or: *a* plus *b* (pause) to the fourth or: *a* plus *b* in parentheses to the fourth	$(a+b)^4$	Klammer *a* plus *b* (Pause) hoch vier oder: *a* plus *b* in Klammern hoch vier
x minus two, times *x* plus three is greater than one.	$(x-2)(x+3) > 1$	*x* minus zwei mal *x* plus drei ist größer als eins.
a prime	a'	*a* Strich
a double prime	a''	*a* zwei Strich
five feet	$5'$	fünf Fuß
five inches	$5''$	fünf Inches
a sub one	a_1	*a* eins
a sub one *x* sub one plus *a* sub two *x* sub two	$a_1 x_1 + a_2 x_2$	*a* eins, *x* eins plus *a* zwei, *x* zwei

Logarithms | ## Logarithmen

logarithm of five with a base *a* or: logarithm five, base *a*	$\log_a 5$	der Logarithmus von fünf zur Basis *a*
logarithm of *x* with a base *a* equals *b* or: logarithm *x*, base a equals *b*	$\log_a x = b$	Der Logarithmus von *x* zur Basis *a* ist gleich *b*.
Natural logarithm of e equals one.	$\ln e = 1$	Der natürliche Logarithmus von e ist eins.
Any positive number can be expressed as a power of 10. The exponent is called logarithm:	$40 = 10^{1,6026\ldots}$ $\log_{10} 40 = 1,6026\ldots$	Jede positive Zahl kann als Potenz von 10 dargestellt werden. Der Exponent wird Logarithmus genannt:

```
           1.6026..
          /      \
   characteristic  mantissa
```

```
           1,6026...
          /      \
      Kennzahl  Mantisse
     (Charakteristik)
```

Ratios, Proportions | | | # Verhältnisse, Proportionen

ratio of a to b	$a:b \quad \dfrac{a}{b}$	Verhältnis a zu b
a is directly proportional to b.	$a = k\,b$	a ist direkt proportional zu b. a und b stehen im direkten (geraden) Verhältnis zueinander.
a is indirectly (inversely) proportional to b.	$a = \dfrac{k}{b}$	a ist indirekt proportional zu b. oder: a und b stehen im indirekten (umgekehrten) Verhältnis zueinander.
Proportion: a is to b as c is to d.	$a:b = c:d$	Proportion (Verhältnisgleichung): a verhält sich zu b wie c zu d.
arithmetic mean	$\dfrac{a+b}{2}$	arithmetisches Mittel
geometric mean	$\sqrt{a\cdot b}$	geometrisches Mittel
harmonic mean	$\dfrac{2\,a\cdot b}{a+b}$	harmonisches Mittel

Percent | Prozentrechnung

Percent means per hundred. % Prozent bedeutet „von Hundert".
60 % of 85 equals 51.   60 % von 85 ist 51.
  60 % (= .60) ... rate   60 ... Prozentsatz
  85 ... base   85 ... Grundwert
  51 ... part   51 ... Prozentwert

Calculation of Interest | Zinsenrechnung

Simple interest: | Einfache Zinsen:
The principal is constant. | Das Kapital ist konstant.

Interest equals principal times rate times time.
$$I = p \times r \times t$$
$$Z = \dfrac{K\cdot p \cdot t}{100}$$
Zinsen sind gleich Kapital mal Prozent mal Zeit dividiert durch 100.

I ... interest
p ... principal (constant)
r ... rate of interest (% annual)
t ... time in years

Z ... Zinsen
K ... Kapital (konstant)
p ... Zinssatz (Prozentsatz p.a.)
t ... Zeit in Jahren

Compound Interest: | Zinseszinsen:
The principal is not constant. | Das Kapital bleibt nicht konstant.

Compound interest (after n years) equals the original principal times the quantity one plus i over one hundred, taken to the nth power.

$$I_n = p\cdot\left(1 + \dfrac{i}{100}\right)^n$$

$$E_n = K\left(1 + \dfrac{p}{100}\right)^n$$

Das Endkapital (nach n Jahren) ist gleich dem Anfangskapital multipliziert mit dem Klammerausdruck eins plus p gebrochen durch hundert hoch n.

p ... principal
I_n ... compound yields
$i\,\%$ ... interest rate (annual)
n ... time (in years)

K ... Anfangskapital
E_n ... Endkapital nach n Jahren
p ... Zinssatz
n ... Zeit (in Jahren)

Expressions and Equations

Terme und Gleichungen

Expression:
a mathematical phrase involving letters, numbers and operation symbols.

$5;\ 3a;\ 4x + 1$

Term:
ein mathematischer Ausdruck (eindeutig), der Buchstaben, Zahlen und Operationszeichen enthalten kann.

Equation in the variable x:
Two expressions involving the same variable x are equated.

$6x + 3 = 2x - 9$

Gleichung in der Variablen x:
Zwei Terme, die die Variable enthalten (können), werden gleichgesetzt.

literal equation

$3bx + ax = 2b$

Gleichung mit allgemeinen Koeffizienten (Formvariablen)

Domain D:
The set of all possible values of the variable of an equation.

Definitionsmenge D:
Die Menge aller möglichen Werte der Variablen einer Gleichung.

The Quadratic Equation:
standard form of quadratic equation

$ax^2 + bx + c = 0$

Die quadratische Gleichung:
allgemeine quadratische Gleichung

Quadratic formula:
x equals minus b plus or minus the square root of b squared minus four ac all over two a.

$$x = \frac{-b \pm \sqrt{b^2 - 4ac}}{2a}$$

Lösungsformel:
x ist gleich minus b plus oder minus Wurzel aus b Quadrat minus vier ac dividiert durch zwei a.

The discriminant gives information about the roots.

$b^2 - 4ac$

Die Diskriminante gibt Auskunft über die Lösungen.

The solution set consists of the two solutions x_1 and x_2.

$L = \{x_1, x_2\}$

Die Lösungsmenge besteht aus den zwei Lösungen x_1 und x_2.

System of linear equations in two variables:
a sub one x plus b sub one y equals c sub one. a sub two x plus b sub two y equals c sub two.

$a_1 x + b_1 y = c_1$
$a_2 x + b_2 y = c_2$

Lineares Gleichungssystem in zwei Variablen:
a eins x plus b eins y ist gleich c eins. a zwei x plus b zwei y ist gleich c zwei.

Matrix:
A rectangular array of elements set out in rows and columns.

Matrix:
Ein rechteckiges Schema von Elementen, die in Zeilen und Spalten angeordnet sind.

A is a 2-by-3 matrix
or: a 2×3 matrix (2 rows and 3 columns)

$$A = \begin{pmatrix} a_1 & b_1 & c_1 \\ a_2 & b_2 & c_2 \end{pmatrix}$$

A ist eine zwei, drei Matrix (2 Zeilen und 3 Spalten)

determinant of rank two

$$D = \begin{vmatrix} a & b \\ c & d \end{vmatrix}$$

zweireihige Determinante

Functions, Sequences and Series | | # Funktionen, Folgen und Reihen

English	Symbol	German
A **function** f is an unique mapping between the elements of the domain D to the elements of the range.	$f: x \mapsto f(x)$ $x \in D$	Eine **Funktion** ist eine eindeutige Zuordnung von den Elementen der Definitionsmenge D zu den Elementen der Wertemenge.
y equals f of x	$y = f(x)$	y ist gleich f von x
f of x equals the set of all x's such that x is greater than two	$f(x) = \{x \mid x > 2\}$	f von x ist die Menge aller x, für die gilt: x ist größer als zwei
the ordered pair two, five	$(2, 5)$	das geordnete Zahlenpaar zwei, fünf
f equals the set of ordered pairs (x, y) such that y equals two x minus one.	$f = \{(x, y) \mid y = 2x - 1\}$	f ist die Menge aller geordneten Zahlenpaare (x, y) für die gilt: y ist gleich zwei x minus eins.
A sequence of numbers is an ordered set of numbers.		Eine **Zahlenfolge** ist eine geordnete Menge von Zahlen.
finite sequence	$a_1, a_2, \ldots a_n$	endliche Folge
infinite sequence	$a_1, a_2, \ldots a_n, \ldots$	unendliche Folge
Properties of sequences:		Eigenschaften von Folgen:
strictly monotonic increasing monotonic increasing: a sub n is less than or equal to a sub n plus one.	$a_n < a_{n+1}$ $a_n \leq a_{n+1}$	streng monoton wachsend monoton wachsend: a_n ist kleiner oder gleich a_{n+1}.
strictly monotonic decreasing monotonic decreasing: a sub n is greater than or equal to a sub n plus one.	$a_n > a_{n+1}$ $a_n \geq a_{n+1}$	streng monoton fallend monoton fallend: a_n ist größer oder gleich a_{n+1}.
The sequence a_n is bounded above, M is the upper bound.	$a_n \leq M$	Die Folge a_n ist nach oben beschränkt, M ist die obere Schranke.
The limit of the sequence a_n as n approaches infinity is α.	$\lim_{n \to \infty} a_n = \alpha$	Der Grenzwert der Folge a_n für n gegen Unendlich ist α.
A convergent sequence has a limit, a divergent has no limit.		Eine konvergente Folge hat einen Grenzwert, eine divergente hat keinen Grenzwert.
A finite (infinite) **series** is the sum of a finit (infinite) sequence.	$s_n = a_1 + a_2 + \ldots a_n$	Eine endliche (unendliche) **Reihe** ist die Summe einer endlichen (unendlichen) Folge.
Notation with the addition sign: The sum a sub i, from i equals 1 to n, equals s_n	$\sum_{i=1}^{n} a_i = s_n$	Schreibweise mit dem Summenzeichen: Die Summe aller a_i, für i ist gleich 1 bis n, ist gleich s_n

Differential calculus

A real function $y = f(x)$ is continuous at a point a if and only if it is definded at $x = a$ and the limit of $f(x)$ as x approaches a is $f(a)$.

$$\lim_{x \to a} f(x) = f(a)$$

Differentialrechnung

Eine reelle Funktion $y = f(x)$ ist in einem Punkt a stetig genau dann, wenn sie für $x = a$ definiert ist und der Grenzwert von $f(x)$ für x gegen a gleich $f(a)$ ist.

The continuity is a necessary but not sufficient condition for differentiability.

Breaks or discontinuities: pole, jump, gap

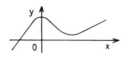

Die Stetigkeit ist eine notwendige aber nicht hinreichende Bedingung für die Differenzierbarkeit.

Unstetigkeitsstellen: Polstelle, Sprungstelle, Lücke

Quotient of differences (slope of a line): $\frac{\Delta y}{\Delta x}$

delta y over delta x
$\Delta \ldots$ symbol for difference

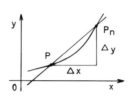

Differenzenquotient (Steigerung der Sekante): $\frac{\Delta y}{\Delta x}$

delta y durch delta x
$\Delta \ldots$ Symbol für Differenz

$\frac{dy}{dx}$ is the limit of $\frac{\Delta y}{\Delta x}$ as Δx approaches 0.

$$\frac{dy}{dx} = \lim_{\Delta x \to 0} \frac{\Delta y}{\Delta x}$$

$\frac{dy}{dx}$ ist der Grenzwert von $\frac{\Delta y}{\Delta x}$, wenn Δx nach 0 strebt.

Derivative of the function $y = f(x)$: dy over dx (slope of the tangent)

$$\frac{dy}{dx}$$

Ableitung der Funktion $y = f(x)$: dy nach dx (Steigung der Tangente)

The first derivative of x^n is n times x to the $(n-1)$th power.

$$y = x^n$$
$$y' = n \cdot x^{n-1}$$

Die erste Ableitung von x^n ist n mal x hoch $n - 1$.

The second derivative:
y double prime equals d squared y over dx squared

$$y'' = \frac{d^2 y}{dx^2}$$

Die zweite Ableitung:
y zwei Strich ist gleich d Quadrat y nach dx Quadrat

Integral calculus

indefinite integral of $f(x)$

$$\int f(x)\, dx$$

Integralrechnung

unbestimmtes Integral von $f(x)$

definite integral of $f(x)$ taken from a to b
   a is the lower limit, and
   b is the upper limit of integral.

$$\int_a^b f(x)\, dx$$

bestimmtes Integral von $f(x)$ von a bis b
   a ist die untere Grenze und
   b ist die obere Grenze des Integrals.

Set Symbols and Logic Symbols / Symbole aus der Mengenlehre und Logik

is the element of	$\in$	ist Element von
is not the element of	$\notin$	ist kein Element von
A is a subset of B	$A \subseteq B$	A ist eine Teilmenge von B
A is a proper subset of B	$A \subset B$	A ist eine echte Teilmenge von B
union of the sets A and B	$A \cup B$	Vereinigung(smenge) der Mengen A und B
intersection of the sets A and B	$A \cap B$	Durchschnitt(smenge) der Mengen A und B
empty set or null set	$\emptyset, \{\}$	leere Menge
disjoint sets	$A \cap B = \{\}$	disjunkte (elementfremde) Mengen
A prime is the complement of set A in set G.	$A' = G \setminus A$	A Strich ist die Komplementmenge von A bezüglich der Grundmenge G.
A is equivalent to B.	$A \sim B$	A ist äquivalent zu B.
A is the set of all x's such that ...	$A = \{x \mid \ldots\}$	A ist die Menge aller x, für die gilt ...
Cartesian product or Cross product of the sets A and B	$A \times B$	Produktmenge (Kreuzmenge, Kreuzprodukt) der Mengen A und B
Set of ordered pairs	$\{(1,2), (3,4), (5,6)\}$	Menge von geordneten Paaren
Negation: not p	$\sim p \qquad \neg p$	Negation: nicht p
Conjunction: p and q	$p \wedge q$	Konjunktion: p und q
Disjunction: p or q	$p \vee q$	Alternative: p oder q
Implicaton: if p then q or: p implies q	$p \rightarrow q$	Implikation: wenn p, dann q oder: p impliziert q
Existential quantifier: there exists ...	$\exists$	Existenzquantor: es existiert ein ...
Universal quantifier: for all ...	$\forall$	Allquantor: für alle ...

Intervals / Intervalle

English	Symbol	Deutsch
closed interval a, b	$[a, b]$, $a \leqslant x \leqslant b$	abgeschlossenes Intervall a, b
open intervall a, b	(a, b) or $]a, b[$, $a < x < b$	offenes Intervall a, b
half open interval (a closed, b open or: from a included to b excluded)	$[a, b)$ or $[a, b[$, $a \leqslant x < b$	halb offenes Intervall (a abgeschlossen, b offen)

Algebraic Structures

Group properties

Example:
Set of real numbers with respect to addition

$(\mathbb{R}, +)$
$a, b, c \in \mathbb{R}$

1. Closure property
The sum of any two real numbers is a real number.

$a + b = c$

2. Associative property
If there are three addends you can combine as shown.

$(a + b) + c = a + (b + c)$

3. Identity property
The number zero is called the additive identity element.

$a + 0 = 0 + a = a$

4. Inverse property
The number $(-a)$ is called the additive inverse element of a.

$a + (-a) = (-a) + a = 0$

5. Commutative property
For any real number a and b the order of addends is interchangeable.

$a + b = b + a$

A group for which the defined operation is commutative is called a **commutative or Abelian group.**

Field Properties

Example: Real field

Set of real numbers with respect to addition and to multiplication

$(\mathbb{R}, +, \cdot)$

1. Commutative group with respect to addition.

$(\mathbb{R}, +)$

2. For every nonzero number: commutative group with resepct to multiplication.

$(\mathbb{R} \setminus \{0\}, \cdot)$

3. Distributive property: combines addition and multiplication.

$a(b + c) = ab + ac$

Algebraische Strukturen

Gruppeneigenschaften

Beispiel:
Menge der reellen Zahlen bezüglich der Addition

1. Abgeschlossenheit
Die Summe von zwei beliebigen reellen Zahlen ist wieder eine reelle Zahl.

2. Assoziativgesetz
Bei drei reellen Zahlen kann man beliebig Teilsummen bilden.

3. Neutrales Element
Die Zahl Null ist das neutrale Element der Addition.

4. Inverses Element
Die Zahl $(-a)$ ist das inverse Element zu a bezüglich der Addition.

5. Kommutativgesetz
Die Reihenfolge zweier Summanden a und b kann vertauscht werden.

Eine Gruppe für die auch das Kommutativgesetz definiert ist, heißt **kommutative oder Abelsche Gruppe.**

Körpereigenschaften

Beispiel: Körper der reellen Zahlen

Menge der reellen Zahlen bezüglich der Addition und der Multiplikation

1. Kommutative Gruppe bezüglich der Addition.

2. Für alle von Null verschiedenen Zahlen: kommutative Gruppe bezüglich der Multiplikation.

3. Distributivgesetz: vereinigt die Addition und die Multiplikation.

Statistics

population	N	
population size		
sample: set of individuals (events) selected from a population		
sample size	n	

Frequency

The absolute frequency is the number of occurrences of an event with some property.

$$n_j \quad j = 1, 2, \ldots k$$
$$n_1 + n_2 + \ldots + n_k = n$$

The relative frequency is the ratio of the absolute frequency to the total sample size n.

$$h_j = \frac{n_j}{n}$$

A **Histogram** is a chart that represents a frequency distribution consisting of rectangles. The height of each rectangle is proportional to the frequency.

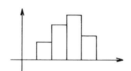

Measures of central tendency
locate the center of a distribution.

The **arithmetic mean** is the sum of a set of data divided by the number of data.

$$\bar{x} = \frac{1}{n} \sum_{i=1}^{n} x_i$$

The **median** m is the value in the middle position in the set of measurements ordered from the smallest to the largest.

$$x_1, x_2, x_3, x_4, x_5$$
$$\uparrow$$
$$m$$

The **mode** is the most frequently occurring value in a set of data.

Measures of variability or dispersion

The **range** of a set of n measurements is the difference between the largest and the smallest.

$$R = x_{\max} - x_{\min}$$

The **variance of a sample** of n measurements equals the sum of the squares of the deviations of the measurements about their means divided by $(n-1)$.

$$s^2 = \frac{1}{n-1} \sum_{i=1}^{n} (x_i - \bar{x})^2$$

The **standard deviation** of a set of measurements is equal to the positive square root of the variance.

$$s = \sqrt{s^2}$$

Statistik

Grundgesamtheit
Umfang der Grundgesamtheit
Stichprobe: Menge von Einheiten (Ereignissen), die aus der Grundgesamtheit entnommen werden
Umfang der Stichprobe

Häufigkeit

Die absolute Häufigkeit gibt an, wie oft ein bestimmtes Ergebnis in einer Beobachtungsserie auftritt.

Die relative Häufigkeit ist der Quotient aus der absoluten Häufigkeit n_j und dem Stichprobenumfang n.

Ein **Histogramm** ist eine grafische Darstellung der Häufigkeitsverteilung durch Rechtecke. Die Höhe jedes Recktecks ist direkt proportional zur Häufigkeit.

Kenngrößen der Lage legen das Zentrum einer Verteilung fest.

Das **arithmetische Mittel** ist die Summe der Menge von Meßwerten dividiert durch ihre Anzahl.

Der **Median** (Zentralwert) m ist der Wert in der Mitte einer der Größe nach geordneten Menge von Meßwerten.

Der **Modus** ist der am häufigsten vorkommende Wert in einer Menge von Daten.

Kenngrößen der Streuung

Die **Spannweite** von n Meßgrößen ist die Differenz zwischen dem größten und dem kleinsten Wert.

Die **Varianz einer Stichprobe** von n Meßgrößen ist die Summe der Quadrate der Abweichungen der Meßgrößen von ihrem Mittelwert dividiert durch $(n-1)$.

Die **Standardabweichung** einer Stichprobe ist gleich der positiven Quadratwurzel aus der Varianz.

Combinatorial analysis

A **permutation** of n objects is an arrangement of these objects into a particular order.

$P(n)$ is the number of permutations of n different objects.
$$P(n) = n!$$

n factorial equals the product of the first n natural numbers.
$$n! = 1 \cdot 2 \cdot \ldots \cdot n$$

Each selection of k objects of a set with n different elements (without respect to the order) is called a **combination** of n objects taken k at a time.
$$C(n, k)$$

$C(n, k)$ is the number of combinations of n objects taken k at a time (read: n over k).
$$C(n, k) = \binom{n}{k}$$

Probability calculation

Sample space:
set of all possible outcomes in an experiment

Event:
particular outcome of an experiment

$P(E)$ is the probability of an event E.
$$P(E)$$

Given a sample space having n equally likely outcomes and s ways for a particular event to occur, the probability of that event occurring is the quotient s over n.
$$P(E) = \frac{s}{n}$$
$$(0 \leq s \leq n)$$

$$0 \leq P \leq 1$$

certain event $\quad P(E) = 1$
impossible event $\quad P(E) = 0$

Kombinatorik

Eine **Permutation** von n Elementen ist eine Anordnung dieser Elemente in einer bestimmten Reihenfolge.

$P(n)$ ist die Anzahl der Permutationen von n verschiedenen Elementen.

n Faktorielle ist gleich dem Produkt der natürlichen Zahlen von 1 bis n.

Jede Auswahl von k Elementen aus einer Menge mit n verschiedenen Elementen (ohne Rücksicht auf die Reihenfolge) heißt eine **Kombination** von n Elementen zur k-ten Klasse.

$C(n, k)$ ist die Anzahl der Kombinationen von n Elementen zur k-ten Klasse (sprich: n über k).

Wahrscheinlichkeitsrechnung

Stichprobenraum:
Menge aller möglichen Ergebnisse eines Experiments

Ereignis:
spezielles Ergebnis eines Experiments

$P(E)$ ist die Wahrscheinlichkeit, daß ein Ereignis E bei einem Zufallsexperiment eintritt.

Bedeutet n die Anzahl aller gleich möglichen Fälle eines Experiments und s die Anzahl der Fälle, bei denen ein bestimmtes Ereignis eintritt, dann ist die Wahrscheinlichkeit dieses Ereignisses der Quotient von s durch n.

sicheres Ereignis
unmögliches Ereignis

Line, Line Segment, Ray | Gerade, Strecke, Strahl

$\overleftrightarrow{AB}$ ... line AB		$g(AB)$ ... Gerade durch A und B
$\overline{AB}$ ... line segment AB		AB ... Strecke AB
AB ... length of segment AB		$\overline{AB}$ ... Länge der Strecke AB
$AB = 2$ cm		$\overline{AB} = 2$ cm
$\vec{AB}$ ... vector (arrow) from A to B		$\vec{AB}$ ... Vektor (Pfeil) von A nach B
ray or half-line with the endpoint A		Strahl mit A als Anfangspunkt

Equality of line segments | Gleichheit von Strecken

The measure of AB is equal to the measure of CD:
$$AB = CD$$
or:
The segment AB is congruent to the segment CD: $\overline{AB} \cong \overline{CD}$

Die Strecken AB und CD sind gleich lang:
$$\overline{AB} = \overline{CD}$$
Beachte:
Der Ausdruck „kongruente Strecken" ist im deutschsprachigen Raum nicht üblich.

Position of lines | Lage von Geraden zueinander

Parallel lines (in the plane) are lines that do not intersect.

Parallele Geraden (in der Ebene) haben keinen gemeinsamen Schnittpunkt.

identical (overlapping) lines

identische (zusammenfallende) Geraden

Intersecting lines are lines that have exactly one common point P.

Schneidende Gerade haben genau einen gemeinsamen Punkt P.

Perpendicular lines form four right angles at their point of intersection, symbol ⌐.

Aufeinander normalstehende (senkrechtstehende) Geraden schneiden einander unter einem rechten Winkel, Zeichen ⌐.

Skew lines are not parallel and not intersecting. They are not in the same plane.

Windschiefe Geraden sind nicht parallel und haben auch keinen Schnittpunkt. Sie liegen nicht in derselben Ebene.

Directions | Richtungen

horizontal
vertical
slanting or skew

horizontal (waagrecht)
vertikal (senkrecht)
schräg (schief)

Angles / Winkel

An angle is formed by two rays (sides) with a common endpoint (vertex).

Notation: $\angle ASB$ or $\angle S$ or $\angle \alpha$

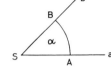

Ein Winkel wird von zwei Strahlen (Schenkeln) mit einem gemeinsamen Ausgangspunkt (Scheitel) gebildet.

Schreibweise:
$\sphericalangle ASB = \sphericalangle (a,b) = \alpha$

Measure: A common unit used to measure angles is the degree (°).

$m \angle ASB$ (measure of angle ASB)
$m \angle ASB = 45°$ or: $m \angle S = 45°$
or: $\alpha = 45°$

Maßeinheit: Eine gebräuchliche Einheit zur Winkelmessung ist der Grad (°).

$\sphericalangle ASB = \alpha = 45°$
Üblicherweise wird in der Bezeichnung nicht zwischen dem Winkel und dem Winkelmaß unterschieden.

Equality of angles / Gleichheit von Winkeln

Angle A is congruent to angle B:
$\angle A \cong \angle B$
or:
The measure of angle A is equal to the measure of angle B:
$m \angle A = m \angle B$

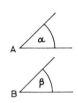

Der Winkel α ist gleich groß wie der Winkel β:
$\alpha = \beta$
Beachte: Der Ausdruck „kongruente Winkel" ist im deutschsprachigen Raum nicht üblich.

Classification of angles / Einteilung der Winkel

zero angle	$\alpha = 0°$	Nullwinkel
acute angle	$0° < \alpha < 90°$	spitzer Winkel
right angle	$\alpha = 90°$	rechter Winkel
obtuse angle	$90° < \alpha < 180°$	stumpfer Winkel
straight angle	$\alpha = 180°$	gestreckter Winkel
reflex angle	$180° < \alpha < 360°$	erhabener (überstumpfer) Winkel
complete rotation	$\alpha = 360°$	voller Winkel

Pairs of angles / Winkelpaare

Two angles whose sum is 90° are complementary. $\alpha + \beta = 90°$
Zwei Winkel, die einander zu 90° ergänzen, sind komplementär.

Two angles whose sum is 180° are supplementary. $\alpha + \beta = 180°$
Zwei Winkel, die einander zu 180° ergänzen, sind supplementär.

adjacent angles α, β
(sharing the vertex)

opposite angles α, γ
(sharing the vertex)

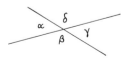

Nebenwinkel α, β
(gemeinsamer Scheitel)

Scheitelwinkel α, γ
(gemeinsamer Scheitel)

Congruence and Similarity

Congruence

Figures having the same shape and the same size.

Triangle *ABC* is congruent to triangle *DEF*.

$\triangle ABC \cong \triangle DEF$

Kongruenz und Ähnlichkeit

Kongruenz

Figuren haben gleiche Gestalt und gleiche Größe.

Das Dreieck *ABC* ist kongruent zum Dreieck *DEF*.

Similarity

Figures having the same shape but not the same size.

Triangle *ABC* is similar to triangle *GHI*.

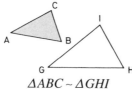

$\triangle ABC \sim \triangle GHI$

Ähnlichkeit

Figuren haben gleiche Gestalt, aber nicht die gleiche Größe.

Das Dreieck *ABC* ist ähnlich zum Dreieck *GHI*.

Scale

"one to two hundred"
1 cm is equivalent to 200 cm

1 : 200
1 cm : 200 cm
1 cm ≙ 200 cm

Maßstab

„eins zu zweihundert"
1 cm entspricht 200 cm

Golden section (ratio)

P divides $\overline{AB}$ in the Golden ratio: The length of the whole line segment is to the length of the larger part as the length of the larger part to the length of the smaller.

$$\frac{AB}{AP} = \frac{AP}{PB}$$

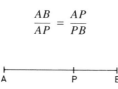

Goldener Schnitt

P teilt *AB* nach dem Goldenen Schnitt: Die Länge der gesamten Strecke verhält sich zur Länge des größeren Teilabschnitts wie die Länge des größeren Teilabschnitts zur Länge des kleineren.

Circle

A circle is the set of all points in a plane that are the same distance *r* from a given point *O*.

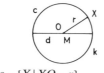

   c ... circle
   O ... center
   r ... radius
   d ... diameter

$c = \{X \mid XO = r\}$
$k = \{X \mid \overline{XM} = r\}$

Kreis

Der Kreis ist die Menge aller Punkte der Ebene, die von einem festen Punkt *M* den gleichen Abstand *r* haben.

   k ... Kreis (Linie)
   M ... Mittelpunkt
   r ... Radius
   d ... Durchmesser

Circumference of a circle (perimeter of a circle)

$C = 2\pi r \qquad U = 2r\pi$

Umfang des Kreises

Area of a circle

$A = \pi r^2$

Flächeninhalt des Kreises

$\overset{\frown}{AB}$ ... arc of a circle
$\overline{AB}$ ... chord of a circle
sector of a circle
segment of a circle

$\overset{\frown}{AB}$ ... Kreisbogen *b*
$\overline{AB}$ ... Sehne *s*
Kreissektor (Kreisausschnitt)
Kreissegment (Kreisabschnitt)

Concentric circles are circles which share the same center.

Two concentric circles form an annulus (ring).

Konzentrische Kreise haben einen gemeinsamen Mittelpunkt.

Zwei konzentrische Kreise bilden einen Kreisring.

Circle and line

I ... non-intersecting
II ... tangent (line)
III ... secant (line)
T ... tangent point
S_1, S_2 ... points of intersection
$t \perp r$ The tangent is perpendicular to radius.

$\overline{S_1 S_2}$ is a chord of the circle

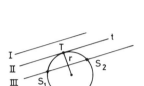

Kreis und Gerade

I ... Passante
II ... Tangente
III ... Sekante
T ... Berührungspunkt
S_1, S_2 ... Schnittpunkte
$t \perp r$ Die Tangente steht normal (senkrecht) auf dem Berührungsradius.

$S_1 S_2$ ist eine Sehne des Kreises

Triangles

Dreiecke

Classification of Triangles

A **scalene triangle** has three sides of unequal length.

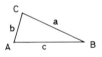

Einteilung der Dreiecke

Ein **ungleichseitiges Dreieck** hat drei verschieden lange Seiten.

An **isosceles triangle** has two sides of equal length: $a = b$.
The base angles (which are equal) are the angles opposite the equal sides.

Ein **gleichschenkliges Dreieck** hat zwei gleich lange Seiten: $a = b$. Die Basiswinkel (die gleich groß sind) liegen gegenüber der gleich langen Seiten (Schenkeln).

An **equilateral triangle** has three sides of equal length: $a = b = c$ (and therefore also three equal angles, equiangular).
The measure of each angle is 60°.

Ein **gleichseitiges Dreieck** hat drei gleich lange Seiten: $a = b = c$ (und daher auch drei gleich große Winkel).
Jeder Winkel beträgt 60°.

An **acute triangle** has three acute angles.

Ein **spitzwinkliges Dreieck** hat drei spitze Winkel.

An **obtuse triangle** has one obtuse angle and two acute angles.

Ein **stumpfwinkliges Dreieck** hat einen stumpfen und zwei spitze Winkel.

A **right-angled triangle** *(Brit.)* or a **right triangle** *(Am.)* has one right angle.
$\overline{AC}, \overline{BC}$ ... legs or sides
$\overline{AB}$ ... hypotenuse

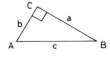

Ein **rechtwinkliges Dreieck** hat einen rechten Winkel.

$BC = a$, $AC = b$ ... Katheten
$AB = c$ ... Hypotenuse

Pythagorean Theorem

In a right (angled) triangle, the square of the length of the hypotenuse is equal to the sum of the squares of the lengths of the legs.

$$a^2 + b^2 = c^2$$

Pythagoreischer Lehrsatz

In jedem rechtwinkligen Dreieck ist die Summe der Flächeninhalte der Kathetenquadrate gleich dem Flächeninhalt des Hypotenusenquadrats.

Lines and Points in a Triangle

Altitude

a perpendicular line segment from a vertex to the opposite side

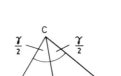

Linien und Punkte im Dreieck

Höhe

eine Normale (Senkrechte) auf eine Seite durch den gegenüberliegenden Eckpunkt

Orthocenter: point of intersection of altitudes

Höhenschnittpunkt: Schnittpunkt der Höhenlinien

Angle bisector

a line segment bisecting an angle of the triangle having its endpoints on the vertex and the opposite side.

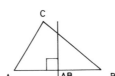

Winkelsymmetrale (Winkelhalbierende)

eine Gerade, die den Winkel halbiert

Incenter: point of intersection of the angle bisectors
inradius: r

Inkreismittelpunkt: Schnittpunkt der Winkelsymmetralen
Inkreisradius: r

Perpendicular bisector of a side

a line perpendicular to the side at its midpoint

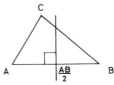

Seitensymmetrale (Mittelsenkrechte)

eine Normale durch den Mittelpunkt der Seite

Circumcenter: point of intersection of perpendicular bisector of sides
circumradius: R

Umkreismittelpunkt: Schnittpunkt der Seitensymmetralen

Umkreisradius: r_u

Median

a line segment joining the vertex of a triangle to the midpoint of the opposite side

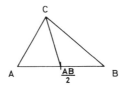

Schwerlinie (Seitenhalbierende)

eine Strecke, die den Eckpunkt eines Dreiecks mit dem Mittelpunkt der gegenüberliegenden Seite verbindet

Centroid: point of intersection of medians

Schwerpunkt: Schnittpunkt der Schwerlinien

Quadrilaterals

Classification of Quadrilaterals

Parallelogram
a quadrilateral whose opposite sides are parallel

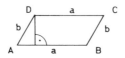

Rhombus
a parallelogram having four sides of equal length

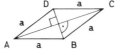

Rectangle
a parallelogram having four right angles

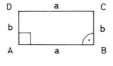

Square
a rectangle having four sides of equal length

Trapezoid *(Am.)*, trapezium *(Brit.)*
a quadrilateral having only two sides parallel

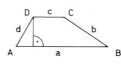

isosceles trapezoid:
$\overline{AD} \cong \overline{BC}$
the non-parallel sides are equal

Kite:
a quadrilateral having two pairs of adjacent sides of equal length

Polygons

A polygon is a closed plane figure bounded by line segments joined at their endpoints.

Regular Polygon
a polygon all of whose sides and angles are equal (congruent)

Vierecke

Einteilung der Vierecke

Parallelogramm
ein Viereck, dessen gegenüberliegende Seiten parallel sind

Rhombus (Raute)
ein Parallelogramm mit vier gleich langen Seiten

Rechteck
ein Parallelogramm mit vier rechten Winkeln

Quadrat
ein Rechteck mit vier gleich langen Seiten

Trapez
ein Viereck mit nur einem Paar paralleler Seiten

gleichschenkliges Trapez:
$AD = BC$
die nicht parallelen Seiten sind gleich lang

Deltoid (Drachenviereck):
ein Viereck mit zwei Paar gleich langer Nachbarseiten

Vielecke (Polygone)

Ein Polygon ist eine ebene Figur mit endlich vielen geradlinigen Begrenzungsstrecken als Seiten.

Regelmäßiges Polygon
ein Polygon mit gleich langen Seiten und gleich großen Innenwinkeln

Geometric solids / Geometrische Körper

Fundamentals / Grundbegriffe

Rectangular Solid / Quader

A rectangular solid is a six-sided prism whose faces are all rectangles.	Ein Quader ist ein Prisma, das von sechs Rechtecken begrenzt wird.

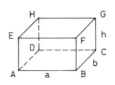

skew projection of a rectangular solid — Schrägriß eines Quaders

vertices	$A, B, C, \ldots$	Eckpunkte
edges:		Seitenkanten:
length	$\overline{AB} = a = AB$	Länge
width	$\overline{BC} = b = BC$	Breite
height	$\overline{AE} = h = AE$	Höhe
faces	$\square\,ABCD, \square\,BCGF, \ldots$	Flächen
diagonal of the base	$\overline{AC} = d = AC$	Diagonale der Grundfläche (Flächendiagonale)
diagonal of the solid	$\overline{AG} = d \qquad AG = d_r$	Raumdiagonale

The two bases are congruent rectangles. — Grundfläche und Deckfläche sind kongruente Rechtecke.

The lateral faces form the lateral area. Two opposite faces are congruent rectangles. — Die Seitenflächen bilden den Mantel (die Mantelfläche). Je zwei gegenüberliegende Seitenflächen sind kongruente Rechtecke.

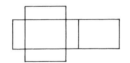

Formulas / Formeln

base	$B = ab = G$	Grundfläche
lateral area	$LA = 2ah + 2bh = M$	Mantelfläche
surface area	$SA = 2B + LA$ $O = 2G + M$	Oberfläche
volume	$V = abh$	Volumen

Classification of solids / Einteilung der Körper

(right) Prism / (gerades) Prisma

a solid figure with plane faces. Its bases are bounded by any congruent polygons and its lateral faces are bounded by rectangles.

ein (geometrischer) Körper, der von ebenen Flächen begrenzt wird. Grund- und Deckfläche sind kongruente Vielecke, die Seitenflächen sind Rechtecke.

$h \ldots$ height / $h \ldots$ Höhe

Cube / Würfel

a special prism. Its faces are congruent squares. — ein spezielles Prisma. Alle Flächen sind Quadrate.

Oblique prism (Parallelepiped)

a prism whose lateral edges are not perpendicular to the base, the lateral faces are parallelograms.

Schiefes Prisma (Parallelepiped)

Seitenkanten stehen nicht normal auf der Grundfläche, Seitenflächen sind Parallelogramme.

(right, circular) Cylinder

a solid figure whose bases are bounded by congruent circles. The lateral area is curved.

  r ... radius
  h ... height

(gerader Kreis-) Zylinder

ein (geometrischer) Körper, dessen Grundfläche und Deckfläche kongruente Kreise sind. Der Mantel ist eine gekrümmte Fläche.

  r ... Radius
  h ... Höhe

(right) Pyramid

a solid figure with plane faces. Its base is bounded by any polygon. The pyramid has a vertex. The lateral area is bounded by isosceles triangles.

(gerade) Pyramide

ein (geometrischer) Körper mit ebenen Flächen. Die Grundfläche ist ein beliebiges Vieleck. Die Pyramide hat eine Spitze. Die Mantelfläche besteht aus gleichschenkligen Dreiecken.

Square pyramid

  S ... vertex
  $\overline{AB}$ ... base edge a
  $\overline{AS}$ ... lateral edge
  $\overline{MS}$ ... height h
  $\overline{ES}$ ... slant height s

Quadratische Pyramide

  S ... Spitze
  $\overline{AB}$ ... Grundkante a
  $\overline{AS}$ ... Seitenkante s
  $\overline{MS}$ ... Körperhöhe h
  $\overline{ES}$ ... Höhe der Seitenfläche h_a

(right circular) Cone

a solid figure whose base is bounded by a circle. The right cone has a vertex directly above the center of its base. The lateral area is curved.

  S ... vertex
  r ... radius
  h ... height
  s ... slant height

(gerader Kreis-) Kegel

ein (geometrischer) Körper, dessen Grundfläche ein Kreis ist. Der gerade Kegel hat eine Spitze, die sich genau über dem Mittelpunkt des Grundkreises befindet. Der Mantel ist eine gekrümmte Fläche.

  S ... Spitze
  r ... Radius
  h ... Höhe
  s ... Mantellinie

Sphere

a solid figure formed by all points with the same distance r from a point O that is the center of the sphere.

  O ... center
  r ... radius

Kugel

ein (geometrischer) Körper, der gebildet wird von der Menge aller Punkte, die von einem festen Punkt M den gleichen Abstand r haben.

  M ... Mittelpunkt
  r ... Radius

Calculation with Vectors | Vektorrechnung

A vector is a quantity that has both magnitude and direction.

Ein Vektor ist eine Größe, die durch Betrag und Richtung bestimmt ist.

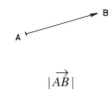

Denotation: $\vec{AB} = \vec{a}$

Schreibweise: $\vec{AB} = \vec{a} = \mathfrak{a}$

Absolute value of the vector (length of an arrow) $|\vec{AB}|$

Betrag des Vektors (Länge eines Pfeils)

Vector Addition | Vektoraddition

If $\vec{OA} = \vec{a}$ and $\vec{OB} = \vec{b}$ represent two vector quantities acting at the same point, then $\vec{OC} = \vec{c}$ is their sum ($\vec{c}$ is the resultant; parallelogram rule).

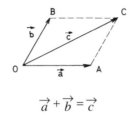

$$\vec{a} + \vec{b} = \vec{c}$$

Sind $\vec{OA} = \vec{a}$ und $\vec{OB} = \vec{b}$ von einem Punkt ausgehende Pfeile, die zwei Vektoren repräsentieren, dann ist $\vec{OC} = \vec{c}$ ihre Summe ($\vec{c}$ ist die Resultierende; Parallelogrammregel).

Vector Subtraction (addition of the inverse vector) | Vektorsubtraktion (Addition des Gegenvektors)

Multiplication of a vector by a scalar ($\vec{a}, \vec{b} \in V$, $\lambda \in \mathbb{R}$)

$\vec{a}$ and $\vec{b}$ are linear dependent (collinear).

$$\lambda \cdot \vec{a} = \vec{b}$$

Multiplikation eines Vektors mit einem Skalar ($\vec{a}, \vec{b} \in V$, $\lambda \in \mathbb{R}$)

$\vec{a}$ und $\vec{b}$ sind linear abhängig (kollinear).

Scalar Product (dot product, inner product) of two vectors that is a scalar. The scalar is equal to the arithmetic product of the magnitudes of the two vectors and the cosine of the angle between their directions.

$$\vec{a} \cdot \vec{b} = \lambda$$

Skalarprodukt (inneres Produkt) von zwei Vektoren ist eine Zahl (Skalar). Sie ist gleich dem Produkt der Beträge der Vektoren und dem Kosinus des von den Vektoren eingeschlossenen Winkels.

Condition of orthogonality $\vec{a} \cdot \vec{b} = 0 \Rightarrow \vec{a} \perp \vec{b}$ Orthogonalitätsbedingung

Vector Product (outer product, cross product) of two vectors that is itself a vector being perpendicular to each of the two given vectors.

$$\vec{a} \times \vec{b} = \vec{c}$$
$$\vec{c} \perp \vec{a}$$
$$\vec{c} \perp \vec{b}$$

Vektorprodukt (äußeres Produkt, Kreuzprodukt) von zwei Vektoren ist wieder ein Vektor, der auf die beiden gegebenen Vektoren normal steht.

Trigonometry

Trigonometrie

The trigonometric functions defined on a right-angled triangle:

Die trigonometrischen Funktionen definiert am rechtwinkligen Dreieck:

Sine (abbreviated sin) that is equal to the ratio of the side opposite the given angle to the hypotenuse.

Sinus (abgekürzt sin) ist gleich dem Verhältnis der dem gegebenen Winkel gegenüberliegenden Seite zur Hypotenuse.

Shorter:

Kürzer:

$$\sin \angle A = \frac{\text{opposite}}{\text{hypotenuse}} = \frac{a}{c}$$

$$\cos \angle A = \frac{\text{adjacent}}{\text{hypotenuse}} = \frac{b}{c}$$

$$\tan \angle A = \frac{\text{opposite}}{\text{adjacent}} = \frac{a}{b}$$

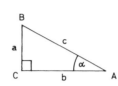

$$\sin \alpha = \frac{\text{Gegenkathete}}{\text{Hypotenuse}} = \frac{a}{c}$$

$$\cos \alpha = \frac{\text{Ankathete}}{\text{Hypotenuse}} = \frac{b}{c}$$

$$\tan \alpha = \frac{\text{Gegenkathete}}{\text{Ankathete}} = \frac{a}{b}$$

The trigonometric functions defined at the unit circle ($r = 1$):

Coordinates of the unit vector $\overrightarrow{OP}$:

$\cos \alpha$ is the abscissa of the unit vector
$\sin \alpha$ is the ordinate of the unit vector

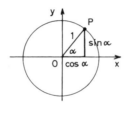

$$\overrightarrow{OP} = \begin{pmatrix} \cos \alpha \\ \sin \alpha \end{pmatrix}$$

Die trigonometrischen Funktionen definiert am Einheitskreis ($r = 1$):

Koordinaten des Einheitsvektors $\overrightarrow{OP}$:

$\cos \alpha$ ist die Abszisse des Einheitsvektors
$\sin \alpha$ ist die Ordinate des Einheitsvektors

Laws in general triangles

Law of Sines
The sides of a triangle are proportional to the sines of the opposite angles:
$a:b:c = \sin \angle A : \sin \angle B : \sin \angle C$

Law of Cosines
is the generalization of the Pythagorean theorem for angles others than 90°:
$c^2 = a^2 + b^2 - 2ab \cos \angle C$

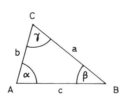

Lehrsätze im allgemeinen Dreieck

Sinussatz
Die Seiten eines Dreiecks sind proportional zu den Sinuswerten der gegenüberliegenden Winkel:
$a:b:c = \sin \alpha : \sin \beta : \sin \gamma$

Kosinussatz
ist eine Verallgemeinerung des pythagoreischen Lehrsatzes, wenn kein Innenwinkel 90° ist:
$c^2 = a^2 + b^2 - 2ab \cos \gamma$

Analytic Geometry

(Coordinate geometry)

Analytische Geometrie

(Koordinatengeometrie)

Cartesian coordinate system

x-axis, y-axis

O is the origin

(a, b) are the cartesian plane coordinates of point P.

Kartesisches Koordinatensystem

x-Achse, y-Achse

O ist der Koordinatenursprung (Nullpunkt)

(a, b) sind die kartesischen Koordinaten des Punktes P im $\mathbb{R}^2$.

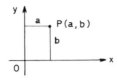

Line in two dimensions

Slope-intercept-form: $y = mx + b$
where m is the slope, and b is the y-intercept of the line.

For the two points $P_1(x_1, y_1)$ and $P_2(x_2, y_2)$ the slope m of the line is the quotient of the differences of the y-coordinates and the x-coordinates.

Gerade in der Ebene

Punkt-Richtungform: $y = kx + d$
wobei k die Steigung und d der Abschnitt auf der y-Achse ist.

Für die zwei Punkte $P_1(x_1, y_1)$ und $P_2(x_2, y_2)$ ist die Steigung k der Geraden der Differenzenquotient der y- und der x-Koordinaten.

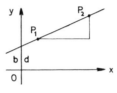

$$m = \frac{y_2 - y_1}{x_2 - x_1} = k$$

Conic sections

They are formed by intersection of a right circular (double) cone and a plane.

Kegelschnittlinien

Sie entstehen durch einen Schnitt eines (Doppel)-Kegels mit einer Ebene.

Circle

A circle is the intersection of a cone with a plane perpendicular to its axis.

For any point P of the circumference the distance to the center is constant.

Kreis

Ein Kreis entsteht durch den Schnitt eines Kegels mit einer Ebene, die normal zur Kegelachse verläuft.

Für jeden Punkt P des Kreises gilt: Der Abstand zum Mittelpunkt ist konstant.

$$\overline{MP} = r$$

Ellipse

An ellipse is the intersection of a cone and a plane oblique to the axis, but not parallel to an element of the cone.

For any point P of the ellipse the sum of the distances to two fix points (foci) is constant.

Ellipse

Eine Ellipse entsteht durch den Schnitt eines Kegels mit einer Ebene, die schräg zur Kegelachse, aber nicht parallel zur Mantellinie, verläuft.

Für jeden Punkt P der Ellipse gilt: Die Summe der Abstände zu zwei festen Punkten (den Brennpunkten) ist konstant.

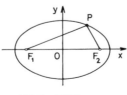

$$\overline{F_1P} + \overline{F_2P} = 2a$$

Hyperbola

A hyperbola is the intersection of a double cone and a plane parallel to the axis of the cone. It consists of two branches.

For any point P of the hyperbola the absolute value of the difference of the distances to two fix points (foci) is constant.

Parabola

A parabola is the intersection of cone and a plane parallel to an element of the cone.

For any point P of the parabola is the distances to a given line (directrix) and a given point (focus) are equal.

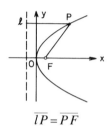

$|\overline{F_1P} - \overline{F_2P}| = 2a$

$\overline{lP} = \overline{PF}$

Hyperbel

Eine Hyperbel entsteht durch den Schnitt eines Doppelkegels mit einer Ebene, die parallel zur Kegelachse verläuft. Sie besteht aus zwei Ästen.

Für jeden Punkt P der Hyperbel gilt: Der Betrag der Differenz der Abstände zu zwei festen Punkten (den Brennpunkten) ist konstant.

Parabel

Eine Parabel entsteht durch den Schnitt eines Kegels mit einer Ebene, die parallel zu einer Mantellinie des Kegels verläuft.

Für jeden Punkt P der Parabel gilt: Die Abstände zu einer gegebenen Geraden (Leitlinie) und zu einem festen Punkt (dem Brennpunkt) sind gleich.

Anhang

Weights and Measures

Linear Measure
1 inch (in) = 2,54 cm
1 foot (ft) = 12 inches = 30,48 cm
1 yard (yd) = 3 feet = 0,9144 m
1 mile = 5 280 feet = 1 760 yards
             = 1,609344 km

Square Measure
1 square inch (in^2) = 6,4516 cm^2
1 square foot (ft^2) = 929,0304 cm^2
1 square yard (yd^2) = 0,83612736 m^2
1 acre = 4 840 square yards
       = 0,4046856 ha
1 square mile = 640 acres
             = 2,589988 km^2

British Liquid Measure
1 liquid pint (liq pt) = 0,5682612 litre
1 quart (qt) = 2 liq pints = 1,1365224 litre
1 gallon (gal) = 4 quarts = 4,5460896 litre
1 fluid ounce (fl oz) = 28,41306 cm^3

American Liquid Measure
1 liquid pint (liq pt) = 0,4731765 litre
1 quart (qt) = 2 liq pints = 0,9463530 litre
1 gallon (gal) = 4 quarts = 3,785412 litre
1 fluid ounce (fl oz) = 29,57353 cm^3

Weights
1 ounce (oz) = 28,34952 g
1 pound (lb) = 16 ounces
             = 453,59237 g
1 ton *(Am.)* = 907,1847 kg = 0,9071847 t
1 ton *(Brit.)* = 1016,047 kg = 1,016047 t

Maße und Gewichte

Längenmaße
1 cm = 0,3937 inches
1 dm = 3,9370 inches
1 m = 1,094 yards = 3,28084 feet
1 km = 0,621504 miles

Flächenmaße
1 cm^2 = 0,1550003 square inches
1 dm^2 = 0,10764 square feet
1 m^2 = 1,19599 square yards
1 ha = 2,4710541 acres

1 km^2 = 247,11 acres = 0,3861022 square miles

Britische Hohlmaße
1 Liter = 1,7597541 liquid pints
1 Liter = 0,8798771 quarts
1 Liter = 0,2199693 gallons

Amerikanische Hohlmaße
1 Liter = 2,1133763 liquid pints
1 Liter = 1,0566357 quarts
1 Liter = 0,264172 gallons

Gewichte
1 g = 0,035274 ounces
1 kg = 2,2046 pounds

1 t = 1,1023114 tons *(Am.)*
1 t = 0,9842064 tons *(Brit.)*

Temperature Conversion

Celsius to Fahrenheit

Multiply the number of Celsius degrees by $\frac{9}{5}$ and add 32:

$$t_{°F} = \frac{9}{5} t_{°C} + 32$$

Fahrenheit to Celsius

Subtract 32 from the number of Fahrenheit degrees and multiply by $\frac{5}{9}$:

$$t_{°C} = (t_{°F} - 32) \cdot \frac{5}{9}$$

Temperaturumrechnung

Celsius in Fahrenheit

Multipliziere die Grad Celsius mit $\frac{9}{5}$ und addiere 32:

$$t_{°F} = \frac{9}{5} t_{°C} + 32$$

Fahrenheit in Celsius

Subtrahiere 32 von den Grad Fahrenheit und multipliziere mit $\frac{5}{9}$:

$$t_{°C} = (t_{°F} - 32) \cdot \frac{5}{9}$$

°C (Celsius)	−20	−17,8	−10	**0**	10	20	40	60	80	100
°F (Fahrenheit)	−4	0	14	**32**	50	68	104	140	176	212

Zahlwörter

Cardinal Numbers *Grundzahlen*

0	nought, null, zero	*null*
1	one	*eins*
2	two	*zwei*
3	three	*drei*
4	four	*vier*
5	five	*fünf*
6	six	*sechs*
7	seven	*sieben*
8	eight	*acht*
9	nine	*neun*
10	ten	*zehn*
11	eleven	*elf*
12	twelve	*zwölf*
13	thirteen	*dreizehn*
14	fourteen	*vierzehn*
15	fifteen	*fünfzehn*
16	sixteen	*sechzehn*
17	seventeen	*siebzehn*
18	eighteen	*achtzehn*
19	nineteen	*neunzehn*
20	twenty	*zwanzig*
21	twenty-one	*einundzwanzig*
22	twenty-two	*zweiundzwanzig*
23	twenty-three	*dreiundzwanzig*
30	thirty	*dreißig*
31	thirty-one	*einunddreißig*
40	forty	*vierzig*
50	fifty	*fünfzig*
60	sixty	*sechzig*
70	seventy	*siebzig*
80	eighty	*achtzig*
90	ninety	*neunzig*
100	a (one) hundred	*hundert*
101	hundred and one	*hundert(und)eins*
200	two hundred	*zweihundert*
1000	a (one) thousand	*(ein)tausend*
2000	two thousand	*zweitausend*
1 000 000	a (one) million	*eine Million*
2 000 000	two million	*zwei Millionen*

Ordinal Numbers *Ordnungszahlen*

1.	first	*erste*
2.	second	*zweite*
3.	third	*dritte*
4.	fourth	*vierte*
5.	fifth	*fünfte*
6.	sixth	*sechste*
7.	seventh	*siebente*
8.	eighth	*achte*
9.	ninth	*neunte*
10.	tenth	*zehnte*
11.	eleventh	*elfte*
12.	twelvth	*zwölfte*
13.	thirteenth	*dreizehnte*
14.	fourteenth	*vierzehnte*
15.	fifteenth	*fünfzehnte*
16.	sixteenth	*sechzehnte*
17.	seventeenth	*siebzehnte*
18.	eighteenth	*achtzehnte*
19.	nineteenth	*neunzehnte*
20.	twentieth	*zwanzigste*
21.	twenty-first	*einundzwanzigste*
22.	twenty-second	*zweiundzwanzigste*
23.	twenty-third	*dreiundzwanzigste*
30.	thirtieth	*dreißigste*
31.	thirty-first	*einunddreißigste*
40.	fortieth	*vierzigste*
50.	fiftieth	*fünfzigste*
60.	sixtieth	*sechzigste*
70.	seventieth	*siebzigste*
80.	eightieth	*achtzigste*
90.	ninetieth	*neunzigste*
100.	(one) hundredth	*hundertste*
101.	hundred and first	*hundertunderste*
200.	two hundredth	*zweihundertste*
1000.	(one) thousandth	*tausendste*
2000.	two thousandth	*zweitausendste*
1 000 000.	millionth	*millionste*
2 000 000.	two millionth	*zweimillionste*

1 000 000 000   a (one) billion *(Am.)*, a (one) milliard *(Brit.)*   *eine Milliarde*

Notizen

Notizen